BOY
SLUT

BOY SLUT

A Memoir and Manifesto

ZACHARY ZANE

ABRAMS IMAGE, NEW YORK

Editor: Zack Knoll
Designer: Heesang Lee
Managing Editor: Glenn Ramirez
Production Manager: Kathleen Gaffney

Library of Congress Control Number: 2022948256

ISBN: 978–1–4197–6471–4
eISBN: 978–1–64700–833–8

ABRAMS The Art of Books
195 Broadway, New York, NY 10007
abramsbooks.com

To Ken,
Thank you for teaching me how to write

TABLE OF CONTENTS

AUTHOR'S NOTE
&
FOREWORD

AUTHOR'S NOTE

Hello my fellow Boysluts,

   While the following stories recount my lived experiences, I did change some folks' names and details to protect their anonymity. There are also some composite characters, meaning a couple of people were mashed up to create one person. I also had to re-create dialogue from memory—really regretting not illegally recording my conversations every time I stepped outside my apartment.

FOREWORD

I've wanted to write this book for quite some time and for a simple reason: I'm not aware of a memoir (or manifesto), written by a bisexual man, about how to overcome sexual shame. Frankly, I think it's about damn time. We are long overdue for more modern, queer, and sex-positive narratives. At the risk of sounding like an asshole, I'm exhausted by the same stories I keep reading: a little gay boy from the South/Midwest who grew up in a religious, homophobic family moves to a big city, finds his chosen family, and learns to embrace who he is. While these *are* important and moving stories, they are just a subsection of the larger queer experience.

Being a greedy bisexual, I wanted more.

I didn't grow up in a homophobic, sex-negative household. I grew up in a very liberal, queer-affirming household—and guess what? I was still overcome with sexual shame. I still struggled with being bisexual, polyamorous, and horny all the time. Sex-negativity is pervasive, insidious, and touches us all—and not in a fun, kinky way. So, as a child and as an adult, I craved narratives that spoke to my experience as bisexual.

Now, according to an impossibly large number of people, bisexuality doesn't exist in men. (*But it totally exists in women and is freakin' hot, man!*) Being told from (ex) lovers, my (ex) psychiatrist, and (ex) friends that a fundamental aspect of my identity wasn't real screwed me up big-time.

Honestly, I find it absurd when people don't think bisexuals exist because we are consistently some of the loudest and most obnoxious people I know. (All we do is make terrible puns while being unable to sit in chairs properly!)

At the same time, there *are* people who believe bisexuality is real—along with a host of negative assumptions about bisexuals: We are incapable of being monogamous; we are greedy; we are in denial; we are whores who spread STIs like they're going out of style. A few of those may be true in my case, but don't prejudge me, asshole!

While I've thought a lot about sex and shame through the lens of my own bisexuality, there's a broader point to make here: Most men do not have a healthy relationship with sex at all. Most women and nonbinary babes don't either, but men, by and large, have been left out of the sex-positivity movement, which is a huge disservice to everyone who ever plans on having sex or simply interacting with a man. While women have seen a shift away from antiquated messages about how to "best please your man" toward something akin to being "strong and sexually empowered," there's little cultural conversation around shifting how men can better engage with and enact their sexuality.

In my sex and relationship advice column at *Men's Health*, Sexplain It, I've tried to play a part in shifting this narrative. I have received countless emails from men across the globe who make it very clear: Men are continuously failing to navigate their sexuality, masculinity, and romantic relationships.

No one wins here. Men are fucked. Women are fucked. Nonbinary angels are fucked. We're all fucked. But hey, that's why I wrote this book. Over the past decade, I've been working on unfucking myself.

While I'm *far* from perfect—I still make mistakes and hurt people despite my best efforts—I have been able to recognize and renounce many of the damaging messages society attempts to ingrain in us. I aim to treat my sexual partners (and the people I reject) with respect, which is somehow still not the norm. I've learned to embrace aspects of my femininity in a manner that doesn't negate my masculinity but complements it. I'm no longer consumed with what I'm "supposed" to do when it comes to relationships. I'm not bound by traditional, hetero-normative scripts; I embrace a range of ethically non-monogamous relationship styles. I've gotten over my sexual insecurities. I'm brazenly out as bisexual, and I don't have a bone in me that's sex-negative. I'm sexually shameless, baby! And all these lessons I've learned? They're sorely needed in our society, arguably more than ever.

How, exactly, have I continuously worked on unfucking myself? Through fucking everyone.* I've had sex with roughly two thousand people. I've had sex with men, women, and nonbinary folks. I've had sex with twenty-one-year-old guys and grandmothers three times that age. I've had sex with people in and from dozens of countries. I've had sex with drug addicts, millionaires, and millionaire drug addicts (free cocaine, yay!). I've had orgies with over a hundred people, anonymous sex in saunas, and have hooked up with my Lyft driver. I've paid for sex and also been paid for sex. I've dommed, subbed, switched, fisted, DP-ed, spit-roasted, tied up, and cuckolded. I've had nipple clamps so tight that my body went into shock and I couldn't feel my face. I've cried during sex and comforted others as they've cried. I've been pegged by a *New York Times* bestselling author, bred contestants from *America's Next Top Model*, boned countless queens from *RuPaul's Drag Race*, and fucked Emmy, Tony, and Grammy winners. I'm working on screwing an Oscar winner to achieve my sexual EGOT.

Of course, I've also had tender, sexual moments with people I've truly cared for—times when all the clichés about sex and love became reality.

Having sex has been the best way for me to learn about sex. But I didn't learn just about sex, I also learned about all the things that sex influences: my sexuality, my manhood, and my relationships with lovers, partners, fuck buddies, friends, family, and, well, the world. Having sex

---

*The sociological term for this is called "being a slut."

helped me unpack the structural systems that idealize an unhealthy masculinity, promote queerphobia, and perpetuate sex-negativity. I believe that if we can understand these systems, we can all unfuck ourselves.

And that is what this book with an absolutely ridiculous, arguably offensive title is all about. *Boyslut* will help you understand the structural systems in place that cause us pain, sadness, anxiety, and anger. It will speak to why so many relationships fail and why a great number of people on this planet are unsatisfied with their sex lives. It will also offer ways to manifest a (sex) life free from these systems while addressing the challenges in having successfully rid yourself of these harmful ideologies. Because guess what? Life is still tough once you have your shit together.

I realize that you may have no desire to sleep with a thousand people, or if you do, you might not have the time or the stamina. Being a slut is a full-time job, after all. (They're paying me to write this book!) The job qualifications include a knack for time management, impeccable communication skills, and an ability to orgasm multiple times a day.

But have no fear if being a slut isn't in your past, present, or future. *Boyslut* is for my fellow sluts to revel in, but it's also for *anyone* seeking to examine their own sexuality and looking to improve and expand their relationships.

Still, don't think of *Boyslut* as a self-help book. Instead, think of it as a memoir and manifesto—a confessional call to arms. It's enlightened smut told by a slutty antihero whose goal in life is to get everyone happily laid—not just for the orgasms, but for bettering humanity.

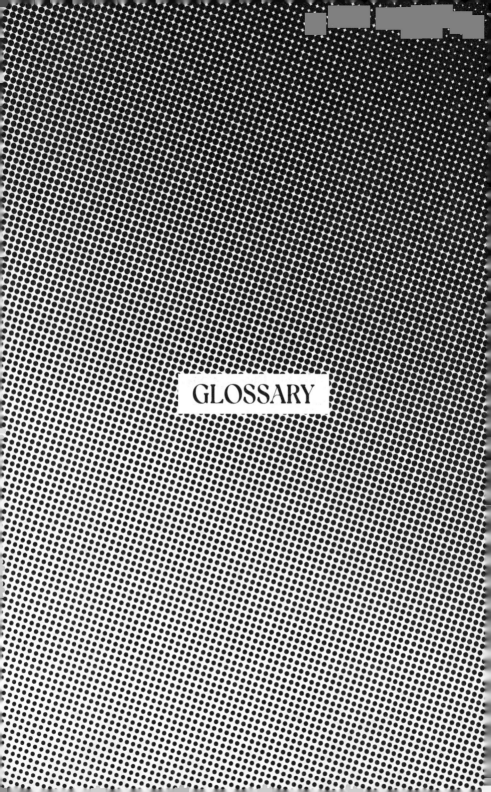

GLOSSARY

I address various topics in this book. I am multifaceted. I have layers! Some of these words, like "fraysexual," you may have never heard before. Others, like "bisexual," have countless definitions, so it can be a little confusing to know what, exactly, I mean when I write these words. I'm sharing here to make sure we're on the same page. Then there are phrases like "ethical non-monogamy," "consensual non-monogamy," and "non-monogamy" that I use interchangeably, and there is a (good) reason why!

Feel free to return to this glossary if you find yourself tangled up in jargon as we deep-dive into the psyche of a thirtysomething, perpetually horny, OCD-ridden bisexual who's made it his life's mission to reduce sexual shame.

BDSM

An abbreviation for bondage/discipline, dominance/submission, sadism, and masochism, BDSM is an umbrella term for a range of sexual practices and interpersonal dynamics. Often it includes elements of roleplaying, power differentials where one is the dominant partner and the other is the submissive, as well as tying someone up.

BISEXUAL

There are many definitions of bisexuality that make understanding the sexual identity a little confusing. From what I've gathered, a lot of the confusion comes from the fact that bisexuality used to refer to attractions to biological sex and not gender. Some folks then changed the definition to indicate an attraction to genders in an attempt to be more inclusive. However, gender is far more nuanced than biological sex, and language cannot fully capture the complexities of gender and sexuality! This leads to inconsistencies and confusion when attempting to define bisexuality (and pansexuality).

That said, a favorite definition of mine comes from bisexual activist Robyn Ochs. She says, "I call myself bisexual because I acknowledge that I have in myself the potential to be attracted—romantically and/or sexually—to people of more than one gender, not necessarily at the same time, not necessarily in the same way, and not necessarily to the same degree."

Ochs differentiates between romantic and sexual attraction, notes that you don't have to be attracted to multiple genders equally, and acknowledges the fluidity of bisexuality—who you find yourself predominantly attracted to right now may change later. Since she focuses on *potential* attraction, Ochs' definition also includes bi people who are monogamous or virgins who have never even kissed someone of the same or different gender. Most important, her definition doesn't perpetuate a gender binary. Some folks think that the "bi" in bisexuality means that you're only attracted to cisgender men and cisgender women. Incorrect! Bi people are attracted to multiple genders, and *most* bi people I've met are indeed attracted to all genders as well as folks who operate outside the gender binary.

While I love Ochs' definition of bisexuality, it is a mouthful. I like to simplify it to: "A person attracted to multiple or all genders." It doesn't have the nuance of Ochs' definition, as "attraction" is so broad, but I think it gets the point across.

BOYSLUT

You might not be thrilled by the title of this book or by the fact that I call myself (and readers) Boysluts. After all, the word "slut" is highly gendered, and it has seldom been hurled at me(n) as an insult intended to harm, belittle, or control my behavior.

Men are often praised for having sex with a lot of women; they're called a player or a regular Don Juan, whereas women are deemed, simply, sluts. This pervasive double standard is not new, and men have always benefited from it. I know I have. Unfairly, women who are called sluts are often deemed either mentally unwell (*she's got real daddy issues*) or undeserving of love (*I'd never marry a slut*).

So why do I feel it's my right to (re)claim a word that hasn't typically been used to hurt and control me? First, I choose to identify as a Boyslut because it exposes the double standard of promiscuity associated with men and women, and, in doing so, hopefully works to dismantle it. Second, as someone who also proudly identifies as a queer faggot, I know the power of reclamation. I hope to help remove some of the stigma and shame that accompanies being a (Boy)slut.

So, what exactly is a Boyslut?

I define it as a person of *any* gender or sexual orientation who approaches sex without a lick of judgment or shame. Being a Boyslut is not about having a high body count; it's about having the sex you want, with whomever you want, however you want, sans shame. Identifying as a Boyslut is to give a gigantic middle finger to society, letting everyone on this planet know that you will not be controlled or behave a certain way just because that's what's considered "normal," "ethical," or "right."

BUSSY

It's BOY pussy, not BUTT pussy. Oh, and I should clarify, "bussy" is what many queer men call their asshole—often ironically or for humorous effect, but sometimes in earnest.

COMPERSION

A word commonly used among polyamorous folks, compersion is the vicarious joy associated with seeing one's sexual or romantic partner having another sexual or romantic relationship that brings them joy. Often compersion is contrasted with jealousy, though, I actually don't think they're opposite sides of the spectrum. I think you can feel both jealousy and compersion simultaneously. Humans are complex, after all.

DEMISEXUAL

People who experience sexual attraction only after they have an emotional connection with someone. Demi people don't see a "hot" person and think, "I wanna sit on their face right now." Only after having a heart-to-heart where they feel safe and emotionally connected do they sometimes desire the aforementioned face-sitting.

DSLS (DICK-SUCKING LIPS)

Very full lips that you *know* would be incredible at sucking a peen. Only a select few were lucky enough to be born with DSLs. The rest of us, myself included, have to get fillers.

ENTHUSIASTIC CONSENT VS. OPT-OUT CONSENT

In short, enthusiastic consent means "'yes' means 'yes!'" Before you ask to touch, hug, kiss, blow, suck, or fuck, you have to get verbal consent from your partner. Anything beyond a "fuck yes!" is a "fuck no!" This contrasts with opt-out consent, which essentially means "'no' means 'no.'" With opt-out consent, it's expected and even appreciated for you to touch without asking.

Typically, gay sex parties utilize opt-out consent (though they don't always explicitly state such). It makes sense. When you're on all fours taking loads, you typically don't want someone to come up and ask, "Can I please insert my penis inside your buttocks?" The whole point is you wanted anonymous loads from strangers who *take* you. While no form of consent is superior, more is left up for (mis)interpretation with opt-out consent. I also take issue with places that don't explicitly state that opt-out consent is being used in their play space. (Swinger parties, *cough cough*.)

ETHICAL NON-MONOGAMY (ENM)

An umbrella term to describe various sexual and/or romantic relationship styles that are not monogamous. The word "ethical" is included to indicate that the people in the relationship are not cheating—all partners are aware and have consented to their partners' extra-coital (and romantic) affairs.

Recently, there has been some pushback on this term from non-monogamous educators, researchers, and activists. They don't like the term "ethical" because it implies that non-monogamy is inherently unethical. (Why else would you feel compelled to preface with "ethical"?) It also holds non-monogamy to an unfair, higher standard than monogamy. Monogamous people constantly lie and cheat on their partners, and they don't have to preface their behaviors with ethical or unethical, so why do non-monogamous folks? Then, of course, many ENM relationships are not ethical. You can absolutely still be a piece of shit even when practicing ENM. For these reasons among others, many educators now opt to use "consensual non-monogamy" (CNM) or simply "non-monogamy."

I'm going to be real with you: This is not a hill I'm willing to die on. I think "ethical" was added to differentiate consensual non-monogamous relationships from infidelity. I think that distinction is important. So, in this book, I use ethical non-monogamy, consensual non-monogamy, and non-monogamy interchangeably.

FRAYSEXUAL

Also known as ignotasexual, this orientation describes someone who is only sexually attracted to someone they are not emotionally connected with; they often lose sexual attraction as they become closer with someone. Fraysexuality is on the other end of the spectrum from demisexuality, or those who are only interested in sex *after* an emotional connection is established. Both fraysexual and demisexual people can be gay, straight, bi, fluid, or any other sexual orientation.

GOLD-STAR GAY

A gay person who's never hooked up with someone of an opposite sex or gender. The term is slightly biphobic, as gold-star gays are often deemed more legitimate or "better" queers for never having had "straight" sex.

L4LS (LIPS FOR LIPS)

Whereas DSLs are big, full lips, L4Ls are slender lips, ideal for kissing, licking, and sucking labia lips. Those with L4Ls can eat pussy like a goddamn pro. Bonus: You don't need fillers!

METAMOUR

In polyamory, a metamour refers to the relationship you have with your partner's *other* partner. So, when I dated a man with a wife, his wife was my metamour, even though I had no sexual or romantic relationship with her.

MOLLY-WOP

The act of dick-slapping someone in the face while receiving a blow job.

MONOSEXUAL

You probably could have figured this one out with your deductive reasoning skills, but it's someone who's only attracted to one sex or gender (i.e., gay or straight people).

OPEN RELATIONSHIP

Someone who is sexually non-monogamous with the consent of their romantic partner. People in open relationships do not have or seek multiple romantic partners.

PANSEXUAL

Someone who is attracted to all genders. Note that pansexuality often denotes the same attractions as bisexuality. I've gathered that the word was birthed out of some confusion about what "bisexuality" meant. Some folks thought being bi perpetuated a gender binary and was exclusionary of nonbinary folks, so they created the term "pansexual," as the prefix "pan" means "all."

Please note that when I say the word "bisexual," which I often do, I'm using it as an umbrella term for all non-monosexual orientations. It's just a little clunky for me to say "bisexual, pansexual, multisexual, omnisexual, ambisexual, heteroflexible, homoflexible, and fluid" every time I bring up attraction to multiple genders.

As of late, I've also seen a new way people define pansexual, which makes a different distinction between being pan and bi. To be honest, I prefer this definition more. Bisexuals are attracted to multiple genders, whereas pansexuals are attracted to folks *regardless* of gender. So in short, pansexuals usually don't take gender into account when looking for a sexual or romantic partner, instead focusing more on other aspects of a person. Bi people, like myself, are attracted to masculinity, femininity, and androgyny. It's not that we don't care about your gender, it's that we're attracted to most or all them sexy genders.

The only "issue" with this definition is that it puts bisexuality and pansexuality at odds. It wouldn't make sense to identify as both bisexual and pansexual, yet many folks do.*

---

*I know this is confusing. Just know that one day I plan on writing a five-thousand-word essay where I really spell all this out and perhaps, just perhaps, offer new definitions. But today is sadly not that day.

PARAPHILIA VS. FETISH VS. KINK

There are distinctions among these three related terms. However, collo-quially, they're used interchangeably, so that's what I do in this book! All three terms refer to sexual desires, objects, and behaviors that fall outside the "norm" of what's deemed by society as "conventional sex." Honestly, what's considered the "norm" is limiting, so most things we do in bed are "kinky." Not to mention that norms differ between cultures and sexual orientations. While it may be considered "kinky" for women to engage in anal sex, it's the predominant form of penetrative sex for queer men.

So, a kink can be anything from being called a "good girl" to spanking, to drinking urine, to sounding, which is when you put a metal rod in your urethra. Needless to say, some kinks are more "intense" than others.

POLYAMORY

Being polyamorous means you're open to the idea of loving multiple people and having multiple romantic relationships simultaneously.* The term "polyamory" comes from the Greek word "poly," which means many, and the Latin word "amory," which means love. Note that polyamory simply means you're *open* to the idea of loving more than one person; a person with one partner can still be polyamorous. You can even have zero partners and be polyamorous!

---

*Throughout the book, I switch between writing "practicing polyamory" and "being polyamorous." Poly folks who view it is a lifestyle choice, one they picked, tend to say they practice polyamory. Those who see polyamorous as a sexual or relational identity say they are polyamorous, similar to the way a gay man says he is gay. He doesn't say he's a practicing gay.

POLYCULE

When you're polyamorous you often have a polycule: everyone who's connected through romantic/sexual relationships. For example, your boyfriend's wife is part of your polycule. So, too, is your boyfriend's wife's girlfriend. Polycules can get large as the web of connections expands, but that's the beauty of it. You end up meeting more people, making new friends, and growing your poly family.

PREP

This is an acronym for pre-exposure prophylaxis. Truvada and Descovy, two FDA-approved forms of PrEP, are two different pills one takes daily to decrease the likelihood of acquiring HIV from sex by 99 percent, and 74 percent among people who inject drugs. Apretude is a new form of FDA-approved PrEP that's administered as two initiation injections one month apart, and then every two months thereafter.

SWINGERS

I'm going to directly quote one of my favorite sex writers in the world, Gigi Engle. In an article for *Men's Health*, she wrote: "Swingers are couples who engage in group sex or the swapping of sexual partners, often at a party hosted by someone in the swinging community. Being a part of this community is called 'being in the lifestyle'—LS, for short. Basically, swingers see their two-person relationships as romantically monogamous and sexually open, meaning they're down to engage in sex with outside partners, while their partner is at the same function (or in the same room)."

Swingers are a specific subset of open relationships, but the term is growing out of fashion among younger communities. Rather than identifying as a swinger, a Millennial or Gen-Zer is more likely to say, "I'm in an open relationship, but my partner and I only play together."

STI VS. STD

You'll notice I use STI (sexually transmitted infection) instead of STD (sexually transmitted disease). That's because gonorrhea, chlamydia, and syphilis are not diseases; they are bacterial infections, just like strep throat. Yet you don't hear people with a strep throat infection saying that they have a disease. Calling sexual infections diseases is a way of stigmatizing sex. In this book, we don't do that!

PART I

SEXUAL SHAME

CHAPTER 1

AM I A SEX-OBSESSED PERVERT?

One of my first memories is imagining my childhood therapist naked. Mark was handsome—the pinnacle of "daddy"—late thirties, solid build, scruffy. He wore floral-printed shirts that were just a small step above Hawaiian.

He had a warm, friendly demeanor, more so than most therapists, perhaps because he worked with children. I suffered from severe obsessive-compulsive disorder, which was why my mom had sought Mark out. His office was cluttered with bright, colorful pictures of cartoon animals sporting supportive phrases, like a penguin who beamed: *You can do anything!* For the last twenty minutes of each session, we always played a game together—at first it was Candy Land, but by the time I left his practice I was beating him at chess.

He usually sat cross-legged, for which I was grateful. Uncrossing his legs meant I would immediately and involuntarily imagine his penis flanked by a big ol' pair of saggy balls. Trying not to imagine his loins only made things worse. *Don't think of his balls. Now I'm thinking of his balls. Balls. Shit, why am I doing this? What's wrong with me? Balls. I'm so messed up. Deep breath. Balls. Now they're closer? I'm such a sicko. Balls. I'm disgusting. Balls. Why can't I stop doing this? Balls. It's because I'm a bad person.* Or, to put it more succinctly: *Balls. Shame. Balls. Shame. Balls. Tears of shame.*

Up until this point, at ten years old, I had seen only one pair of testicles other than my own: my father's. It was never on purpose, yet they always managed to peek out through his robe. To this day, three of my closest childhood friends have accidentally seen my father's testicles, and the verdict has always been the same: *Holy fuck, dude, those are like grapefruits!*

After more than a dozen sessions plagued by images of Mark's massive testicles and silver bush, I felt it was time to confess. Not only was the guilt too much for my prepubescent, grape-size-testicled soul to bear, I also was seeking absolution. That's what people with OCD do. You've probably heard that people with OCD repeatedly wash their hands, but some of us approach cleansing in other ways. We attempt to clean our minds of guilt-inducing thoughts, seeking out relief from guilt that's eating us away. We need to be told explicitly and frequently that what we're thinking is okay, and we're not a bad person for having these thoughts.

I took a deep breath. "I want to say something really bad," I said.

"That's okay! You can share anything you want here. There's never any judgment," he replied.

"But this is *really* bad," I clarified.

"I'm sure it's not as bad as you think."

"Okay," I said, confident Mark was not understanding the full gravitas of the situation. After what felt like an eternal pause, I began to stammer, "I—I—" I had to spit it out: "I imagine people naked. A lot."

His face and demeanor didn't change. He sat there, smiling, as if I hadn't dropped a bomb. Really, like any good therapist, he was just waiting for me to elaborate.

"Everyone," I continued. "Not even people I like. Just everyone. I can't stop it, even though I try."

Finally, he spoke. "It's okay, Zach. We all imagine people naked."

That did not ease my guilt. I didn't care about what other so-called normal people did. I cared about *me* and *my* "bad" behavior.

"I mean everyone," I continued. "Like old people. Kids in school. Everyone. I just can't stop."

It was at that exact moment that Mark uncrossed his legs to reposition.

"Like you," I confessed. "I'm imagining you naked right now."

He laughed, both professional and unfazed, reiterating how I was allowed to imagine anyone naked. Anyone included him. There was nothing "wrong" with that.

"But how do I stop?" I asked, on the cusp of tears. "It's distracting. I can't concentrate on anything else." My gaze kept darting down until I resigned myself to shutting my eyes. Focused as I was on futile attempts to keep him clothed, his response still landed.

"Thinking of people naked isn't bad. You'll only be able to stop thinking of people naked when you truly believe that. When that happens, your thoughts will pass just as quickly as they come. But when you think of something, in this case nudity, as being bad, the thoughts and images won't pass. You dwell on them." My eyes were closed but I imagined him repositioning his hairy grapefruits. "So I'm here to tell you, Zach, that there's nothing wrong with any of your thoughts surrounding nudity. There's nothing wrong with *you*."

I'd only realize later this was Mark's attempt to teach me coping mechanisms for intrusive thoughts caused by OCD. "Talking yourself down," while extremely difficult, is a way to work through intrusive thoughts. CBT (cognitive behavioral therapy, not to be confused with cock and ball torture), a common treatment for anxiety and OCD, is all about this; you attempt to reframe your thoughts while not getting overwhelmed by negative emotions.

Eyes still closed, I nodded while taking a deep breath. When I opened them, Mark was fully dressed. Shoulders back, head held high, I left my shrink's office to where my mom was illegally parked. I felt as if I had accomplished something. I'd no longer see a world filled with naked, flesh-colored zombies whose sole purpose was to make me feel guilty. Even my little preteen self was able to see this "breakthrough" as a momentous occasion.

"How'd it go?" my mom asked as I climbed in.

I looked at her, immediately imagined her naked, and said, "Fine."

X X X

As much as I love to think I'm special, a lot of people with OCD suffer from sexual intrusions and guilt. As I got older, I wondered why my OCD manifested this way. Couldn't I have been a compulsive hand-washer, or an organizational devotee, or a dude who has to turn his lights on and off sixteen times before leaving his apartment? I once stumbled onto a Reddit thread where a father with OCD kept having intrusive thoughts about murdering his own daughter in gruesome ways, even though he loved her and would never do anything to hurt her. Given the endless ways OCD manifests, why did my brain predominantly skew toward sexual guilt?

Religion wasn't the culprit. I grew up in Los Angeles' San Fernando Valley (aka "the Valley"). Both my parents are liberal, Reform(ish) Jews. In case you aren't familiar, Reform Jews are the "chiller" denomination who tend to be more culturally Jewish than strictly religious. Even though I did study the Torah, Talmud, and Mishnah in day school, my parents made it very clear from a young age that we saw the Bible as fiction. It was not the word of God, so I could pick and choose the good parts and let go of the rest. All of the stuff about homosexuality being an abomination? "Honey, you can just skip right over that part!" Mama Zane said. To be honest, I'm happy that religion wasn't the root of my sexual shame because frankly, it's so *basic* to get sexually fucked up by organized religion, and I ain't no basic bitch.

What about the age-old Oedipus complex? Sure, "daddy issues" are very en vogue right now, but Jewish sons are famous for having "mommy issues." Against all odds, I feel certain that my mother wasn't the cause of my sexual guilt either. For one, I'm the third of three boys, and as the youngest child of any family will proudly reveal, you can get away with murder as the baby. Still, I don't want to imply that my mom got lazy. She was a very present figure growing up.[*]

But by the time she got to me, she was much more lax about all things sexual, having visited this rodeo twice before I came of age. My seeing a pair of boobs on TV at twelve wasn't the end of the world. Later, she'd let my girlfriend sleep over, knowing damn well we were fooling around.

We also weren't one of those families who couldn't see one another naked (see: my dad's wandering testicles). If the phone rang while I was taking a poop, I would absolutely have my mom come in and hand me the portable landline. My friends would insist I'd call them back, and I'd explain that if they hung up now, they will have made my mom smell my shit in vain. Did they really want to do that to my kind, innocent mother?

My mom was also quick to see I had severe mental health issues. I exhibited signs of OCD since before I could remember, but she sure could. While sexual guilt was my OCD's go-to mindfuck from ages seven to eighteen, it would whip out some other fun surprises, too. My OCD was the ultimate drag queen—reveal after reveal.

For example, my mom told me she had to get rid of the "punishment chair" in the corner of the living room, where she'd send us kids when we were bad; she'd often find me sitting there when I wasn't sentenced. I would proceed to explain that I'd had a bad thought—I

---

[*]See, Mom, I told you I wouldn't blame everything on you. You get blamed later, when I'm an adult!

wouldn't tell her what it was because it was *that* bad—and would insist I deserved punishment. I was four years old.*

In elementary school, I would accidentally see someone's answer on a test and then convince myself I actually *wanted* to see their answers because I was a worthless cheater. Cut to hours of crying while convincing myself I was a bad person.

My OCD didn't always take the form of mental flagellation either. It's called obsessive-*compulsive* disorder for a reason. In addition to endless, guilt-inducing ruminations (i.e., obsessions), I also couldn't stop engaging in certain physical behaviors (i.e., compulsions). I would use multiple rolls of toilet paper whenever I wiped to ensure I was squeaky clean. This would mean not only taking thirty minutes every time I used the facilities, but also that I would leave with a raw and bloodied asshole.†

In my middle school years, I had trouble sleeping because I'd check my alarm clock every ten minutes to make sure it was still on. It always was. I'd immediately want to check again, reconfirming what I already knew. This led to many sleepless nights, and spending a childhood perpetually exhausted didn't help my problems.

There's a critical self-loathing element that comes with OCD, at least in how my symptoms manifested. As I grew older, I knew my compulsions were ridiculous but still couldn't stop myself. I *had* to wipe my asshole until it bled. I *had* to run back six times to make sure I locked the front door. I *had* to check my alarm every ten minutes to confirm it was still set. My inability to control my actions led to feeling powerless. Eventually, my powerlessness morphed into anger, and there was nowhere to direct it but inward. I would call myself stupid, insane, broken—and I'd believed it.

---

*Somehow punishment is *not* one of my many kinks.
†This *probably* explains why I now avoid douching like the plague.

Well, kinda. I knew I wasn't stupid; but yes, I did feel I was broken, or at least that my brain was.

There was seemingly nothing I could do, since, after all, this was just who I was. This was my brain. And this brain led me to believe my life would always be a string of ridiculous obsessions and compulsions. I'd always be tired. I'd never be able to think straight. I'd always believe I was a bad person. I'd be haunted by strangers' hairy nuts until the end of my days. It's easy to feel hopeless when you're not in control of your own reality. Luckily, my mom recognized that my behavior was unhealthy and swiftly acted. Enter: Mark.

About a year after I started therapy, Mark and his testicles referred me to a psychiatrist. There, I was officially diagnosed with "severe" OCD. And like every psychiatrist, he recommended medication. "Zach, do you want to try these?" my mother asked.

I was crying, but it wasn't your typical ten-year-old wailing. These were quieter tears of exhaustion. I was exhausted from sleeplessness, but also the constant guilt, the constant interruptions.

There was a happiness to the tears, too, a catharsis. These pills were going to *fix* me. For the first time in a long time, I could imagine a world where I was different, where I was normal. I nodded yes.

Her friends judged her and thought she was making a terrible mistake by medicating me. (Though it was my decision, not hers. She offered me agency, and I love the hell out of her for that.) The gaggle of disapproving mothers thought my outrageous behaviors were mere childhood eccentricities. Things I would inevitably grow out of.

I did, for the most part, "grow out of it," but not because my mom ignored the problem. With extensive CBT, 200 milligrams of Zoloft in the morning, and later, 100 milligrams of Trazodone at night, I "grew out of it." Or rather, I worked hard in therapy, prioritized my mental health, and was blessed to have a mother who didn't give a fuck about what her judgmental suburban friends thought.

This took years. During which, I still checked my alarm clock repeatedly throughout the night, just less. I still felt guilty about imagining people naked, just less. I also still hated myself, but this one, a lot less.

X X X

I don't bring up my struggle with mental health to brag. (Just a reminder, my psychiatrist did use the word "severe.") And while no memoir is complete without delving into childhood trauma, that's not why I'm sharing stories of my over-wiped, bloodied asshole either.

I tell you this because my mom knew I had some misplaced guilt and preoccupations surrounding sex. While I didn't want to tell her every single sexual thought I deemed "bad," I often couldn't stop myself. I was so consumed by my obsessive thoughts that I had to tell her, so I could feel absolved. I needed to hear "Zach, that's okay!" in order to function. That's why she actively worked hard not to be sex-negative and attempted to normalize sexual behavior in our household. There was also the fact that she wanted me to fuck everything in sight once I lost my virginity. Not typical advice for your hormonal, teenage son, but words she lived by.

Shortly after I started having sex, I remember sitting on my water-bed* with my first girlfriend. My mom came in and sat down next to us, creating a wave. Both quickly and inorganically she managed to bring up in conversation: "When you break up and start sleeping with other people . . ."

Why the hell would she say that? What was she getting at? I was entering month eight with my girlfriend. We were still head over heels in love with no end in sight to our relationship.

---

*Yes, you may judge me.

When she left the room, I felt compelled to apologize on her behalf. Luckily, my girlfriend was an independent badass who didn't give a fuck about what other people thought—and that included my mother.

"I do find it weird how she openly discusses that we're fucking," she said. I nodded while she continued, "Does she still not like me?"

"Honestly," I said while shaking my head, "I have no idea."

Eight months later, we had the same talk, again on my waterbed, only with my next girlfriend. I still had no clue why. Maybe my waterbed was to blame.

"Well, that was fucked-up," my new girlfriend said within seconds of my mother leaving. "Does she not like me?"

"No, it's not that," I said. "She just does this. I don't know why she's always telling me to be single and fuck everyone."

It wasn't until I was on a flight from Burbank to JFK, heading to college, when I finally learned why she was steadfast in her desire for me to be a Boyslut. Seemingly out of nowhere, my mother put down her trashy romance novel, turned to me, and said, "Just in case I die, there's something about me you need to know."

Immediately I panicked, convinced she had terminal cancer. My mother clarified that she was not dying, she was simply married prior to my father.

"Why are you telling me now?" I asked.

"There was no reason to tell you before, but eventually I will die, and since you're an adult now, you'll see documentation of my first marriage, and I don't want you wondering why I never told you."

I said nothing. I didn't know what to feel and still believed that there must be some health problems.*

---

*That wasn't an OCD thought. There were always health problems in my family, and not just the pair of bowling balls between my dad's thighs.

"I believed you had to marry the man you lost your virginity to," she said, at which point I raised an eyebrow because she sure didn't raise me to think that.

"We were only married for a year," she clarified. "It didn't work out." I didn't press any further. The specifics didn't matter.

I later realized this was why she encouraged—even fostered—my slutty antics. She was afraid I was going to repeat what she felt were her mistakes. It wasn't necessarily that she *wanted* me to fuck everyone, even if that's how I interpreted it. She just wanted me to sleep with and date enough people so that by the time I did settle down, it would be with the right person.*

Well, if Mom's in the clear, what about dear old Dad? I can't say he contributed to my sex-negativity either. Maybe less unexpected, but he was also gung-ho about me sticking my dick in anything that moved.

Starting in college, he would ask in a caring, oddly paternal way if I was getting laid. While this may sound bizarre, once I started dating women in my teens, he wanted to make sure I was having fulfilling sexual relationships. I would answer yes because that was the truth. While I may never have had *the* sex talk with my father, I feel like we had constant talks *about* sex. Their messages were always the same: be safe, prioritize her pleasure, and enjoy it.†

He gave me my first condom when I was fourteen. "I think you're too young to have sex and shouldn't be," he said, "but if you do, use protection." While I didn't have sex for the first time until two years later with my girlfriend, it's incredible to realize how open-minded he was. I'm grateful Papa and Mama Zane had these conversations with me early. They helped normalize sex and sexuality.

---

*This is actually pretty solid advice, Mom!
†I wasn't hooking up with guys *just* yet.

So why, then, the pang of guilt whenever sexy daddy-slash-therapist Mark uncrossed his legs?

X X X

Remember how no memoir is complete without delving into childhood trauma? When I was seven years old, I was caught rolling around naked in bed with a friend. This wasn't the first time we had done this—we had also done this before at his house. I'm not sure exactly what it was we thought we were doing. I just remember smacking his butt and liking it. I also remember enjoying the feeling of rubbing my body up against his. We would roll around in bed and then roll some more. I'd then squeeze parts of his body, and he'd squeeze mine.

This final time we did our naked gymnastics routine, I remember that he voiced some reluctance and wanted us to "play" in my bathroom, where we could lock the door, out of fear of getting caught. I, however, coaxed him to play in my bedroom.

So while we weren't sure what we were doing, we knew it was something that we probably shouldn't be doing. Still, we went to my bedroom, dropped our briefs, and began rolling. That's when my nanny caught us.

Andrea screamed louder than anyone has ever screamed, and I've been in a gay bar where Kim Petras surprised patrons with an unannounced performance. I started crying because of course I did. What I was doing was very, *very* bad, she explained. Something I should never do. Something I should be ashamed of.

When my mom heard screams, she came rushing in, and Andrea told her exactly what she'd seen. She excused Andrea and calmed me (and my friend) down, but the damage was done. My mom wasn't mad. Kids do random shit like this. She understood that we have these strange, little things dangling between our legs that we're constantly told not to touch and show. Everyone seems obsessed with them, but we can't talk about them.

While I was too young then to parse out the complications of same-sex attraction, I came from an extremely queer-accepting household. I actually have queer uncles on both sides of the family—three to be exact. With more than half of my uncles being queer, I knew, even at that age, that not only was it A-OK to be gay, but you could also live a fulfilling life as a queer man.*

Even so, Andrea scarred me. I loved that woman more than anything. I used to go into her room while she slept, so I could cuddle her. I would beg her to feed me her half-eaten food, directly from her mouth like a mama bird.† When she resigned after getting married, I cried for days on end.

She had never yelled at me before, and being yelled at for the first time by someone I loved—and specifically for being intimate with another boy—did not do wonders for my mental health or sexual identity journey. Despite my mother's best attempts to normalize the situation, I convinced myself everything was not all right. That I was bad. That touching boys was bad. That sex with boys was bad. That *anything* sexual was bad.

I don't blame Andrea. She was doing the best she could do and reprimanding me the way she thought was right. She, like us all, was a product of a sex-negative and homophobic society. I'd be willing to bet her Catholic upbringing taught her that premarital sex was wrong, and sex between two men—two boys—was *very* wrong. So seeing the child she was raising, the child she told she loved daily, rolling around naked with another boy? She was just doing what she thought was right.

---

*A few years ago, I drunkenly made a pass at my uncle's ex-boyfriend, whom I still refer to as Uncle Phillip. Rightfully, he turned me down, reminding me that he held me as a newborn. We're still besties though!

†Among having OCD, I was also afflicted with being a spoiled brat.

But sometimes what we think is right—or what we've been taught to believe is right—can be so wrong.

<h1 style="text-align:center">X X X</h1>

It's weird to think that such a relatively innocuous experience at such a young age can have a huge impact on the rest of your life, but it speaks to why no child is safe from societally induced sex-negativity. It's too pervasive, and all it takes is one negative experience to shape your outlook on sex. It may be someone telling you that you are wrong, sick, perverted, or a slut for having (completely normal) sexual desires; it may be someone directly or even indirectly shaming you for being a healthy human who craves intimacy and pleasure. There's no way to get through life without having at least *one* of these formative experiences, and all it takes is one to negatively distort your sense of self.

Which is to say, if Andrea hadn't shared her horror, I'm sure plenty of other experiences would have triggered my sexual shame. Having a fucked-up relationship with sex(uality) was in the cards. It's in the cards for all of us. Maybe you have religion-induced sexual guilt. Maybe your parents were super sex-negative. Maybe they weren't sex-negative as much as they pretended sex didn't exist, so you had to form your own (wrong) conclusions about sex. Maybe you had a sexual health teacher who scarred you. Or your friends screwed you up. Or you simply existed and consumed any of the constant barrage of sex-negative media that's constantly rammed down our throats.*

I was seven when the Lewinsky-Clinton scandal was splashed on the front page of every tabloid. That was how I learned what a blow job was. *That* was the context. My only takeaway was you shouldn't

---

*Not in the hot way.

give blow jobs. As an adult, I can say the much larger takeaway is that if you're a man in a position of power, you can do whatever you want—including seduce a teenager—and you will not be blamed. *She* will be deemed the perpetrator or the villain. *She* will be the "slut." *She* will be bullied relentlessly and be the butt of jokes for decades to come.

I was thirteen when Janet Jackson's "Nipplegate" aired during the Super Bowl halftime show. Despite Timberlake ripping off Jackson's costume, revealing her breast (her nipples were guarded with pasties), he received hardly any flack for the incident. It all landed on Jackson. Once again, here was a man not being held accountable for his actions. And in this scenario, I learned that nudity—if you could even call it nudity with her nipple shields on—is "bad," and even minor forms of sexual expression will be penalized.

I was nineteen when Instagram came out. At first, it allowed sexual education on its platform, but it has since regressed, blocking educators and content creators who are simply trying to provide accurate sexual information. The inability to simply discuss sex, not even in a salacious manner, but educationally, speaks volumes to how society views any talk of sex. Censorship reinforces and perpetuates sexual shame by making it clear that sex in any capacity should never be discussed.

I was twenty-five when Amber Rose, the sex-positive icon who brought international attention to the SlutWalk, said she wouldn't feel comfortable dating a bisexual man. If someone like Amber Rose, a bisexual, self-proclaimed slut, doesn't feel comfortable dating a bisexual man, then bi guys had no chance dating women. I remember hearing her words and feeling hopeless—not shame, but hopelessness; her comments revealed that even the most sex-positive people in the world can't shake their subconscious biphobic beliefs, even when they, themselves, are bisexual.

I wonder what would have happened if I wasn't led to believe that expressing myself with another man was wrong. What would happen if we allowed *all* children not to be manacled by sexual shame at such an early age? We would have significantly healthier romantic and sexual relationships. We would be more open in discussing our sex lives with our partners, addressing what we want sexually and what we don't feel comfortable doing. This would likely cause a drop in infidelity and divorce rates. More people would come out as queer (hello, plummeting rates of alcoholism, depression, anxiety, and suicide). We would also, collectively, be more open to ethical non-monogamy because we'd realize that for many, it's unrealistic for one person to satisfy all our sexual needs. And of course, there would be less slut-shaming, which has been a tool to socially maim, devalue, and control women, specifically.

This is all to say that I believe a world unriddled by sexual shame is a better world for all of us, by any and every metric imaginable.

So what if we not only permitted but somehow encouraged sexual exploration from a young age? I don't mean this in a creepy, pedophilic way, but in a sex-positive nudist colony sort of way. What if we taught children: This is your body, and you have autonomy over it. You, and for that matter, anyone else, can say "no" at any point, and that "no" must be respected. And when you're a little older, you can touch and explore with others consensually. Even from a young age, there must be a way to foster healthier attitudes that normalize sex and facilitate respect.

I wish I could snap my fingers and wipe sexual shame out of our society, but I can't. I'm not even sure how a shame-free utopia would look, or if it can exist at all. But I do know that the first step is honest communication and championing the idea that there's nothing wrong with sex.

I spent most of my late teens and early twenties unlearning what I was taught by society to be "wrong." There's some truth in the cliché that children are sponges. Even though my parents were sex-positive, they weren't enough to combat my traumatic nanny moment, teachers, the messages I soaked up from media, what I learned from friends, and so on. Lord knows having OCD made everything worse and contributed to my many years of confusion, anxiety, sleepless nights, blacked-out sexual encounters, and heartbreaks.

But I've worked toward unlearning shame. First and foremost, I read. (You're doing this now, so you're already on the right track.) We live in the era of information, and you should read any and everything that promotes sex-positivity.

I got into therapy. For the love of God get into therapy now if you're not. I know there are so many godawful therapists, but spend the money or find services that can offer a sliding scale or even free sessions—they're out there. Take the time to find a therapist you connect with. It's the best way to overcome shame because you *need* to talk it out. You gotta delve deep, tackling the root of your shame and insecurities, and that's just something you can't do with a book, excluding, of course, this book, which you spent twenty-six dollars on.

Then I had sex—a *lot* of sex. Each time, I felt slightly more comfortable with my desires, and even more comfortable expressing them. The first time I had sex with a man I felt *very* guilty and confused. By around the hundred-man mark, I wasn't ashamed. Now at the 1,500-man mark, shame is laughable. I'm just out here living my best life. And while having sex with everyone is great, let me tell you what's even better: talking about sex with everyone. Sure, at times it's been awkward. At times I've been rejected, received side-eye, or been called "faggot," "pervert," "disgusting," and so much more. But in talking to people from all walks of life, I've learned that sex and our more "taboo" desires are what unite us. In revealing what turns me on, I'm often gobsmacked by how many people share in my desires.* When it comes to sex, we are not special—and this is a good thing. Every weird kink you have? Thousands, if not millions, of people share it, too.

Shame makes us feel alone. It isolates us. It makes us think we're not lovable or worthy of love, but we are. We're humans, and most primally, we're programmed to fuck, love, and connect.

Now, at the ripe age of ████████, I no longer uncontrollably imagine people naked. I imagine them naked when I *want* to, and I sure as hell don't feel any guilt about it. Well . . . for the most part. Do I still have other intrusive thoughts that appear unexpectedly? Of course. I'm not "cured" of my OCD. There is no cure.

But when I'm masturbating in the shower, and a violent sexual scene mysteriously appears in my mind, I don't spend the next five hours worried about whether I'm secretly a depraved and perverted sicko. I simply shoot my load and carry on with my merry day. Besides, I'm most *definitely* a little pervert, and I wouldn't want to have it any other way.

---

*And just WAIT until you get to chapter 11. I am into some weird shit.

CHAPTER 2

AM I ADDICTED TO PORN?

I n fifth grade, when my best friend Sam called to say that he needed me to run to his house right away, I was really hoping he was going to show me a dead body. While he did show me a lifeless body, it wasn't the kind I was expecting.

Sam was waiting for me at his front door and quickly ushered me inside, checking for a cleared coast before carefully shutting and locking the door behind him.

"What the hell is going on?" I asked.

"Let me show you," he replied.

Whereas I only ever used our shared family computer in my mom's home office, Sam had the luxury of a computer in his bedroom—the kind of privacy a pubescent boy could only dream of. He locked his door and fired up the 56k modem with a chorus of beeps and boops. Approximately fifteen years later—I do not miss the days of dial-up—we were on the emerging World Wide Web. He navigated us to eBaum's World, an entertainment site, which still exists today, that caters to teenage and college-aged bros. He clicked through until we reached a page with an attractive, buxom blonde model wearing a sheer negligee.

"Look," he said, his face inches from the screen. "You can take off her clothes." He removed each article of clothing until she was nude. Her breasts were like cantaloupes, and she had a landing strip in a slightly darker shade of blonde than the hair on her head. I could not look away. *That*—that—*is what a vagina looks like*, I thought.

I quickly got hard, and with it came my bestie *shame*—deep, unrelenting shame. I was still in my hit era of "imagining people naked is bad," but at least that was involuntary. This was a choice. We chose to remove that woman's clothing, and we chose to ogle.

I felt like a creep, largely because the figure was looking away from the camera with a neutral face. It felt like I was undressing her without consent—not that I even knew what the word "consent" meant yet. If she were looking at me with a seductive face, it would have been (slightly) better, but she didn't know what we were doing. She was our two-dimensional Barbie, and that felt especially wrong.

"Woah," I said while closing the browser. I stayed at Sam's for about twenty minutes more before feigning a stomachache. I needed to get out of there. Within minutes, I was crying in my mom's car.

When she asked what was wrong, I, in classic Zach fashion, said it was so bad that I couldn't tell her. But the thing about OCD is that you *have* to share what's on your mind. So when she pushed just a little bit harder, I cracked worse than an eighth-grade choirboy's voice, sharing everything in unnecessarily vivid detail.

My mom tried not to laugh. I think she was expecting something far worse given my preface, so this laugh was also a sigh of relief. When I asked why she was laughing, she said, "No, honey! Everything is okay. What you did was completely normal and healthy."

"It is NOT normal or healthy!" I rebutted. "What we did was bad."

My mother then explained that Sam was at a different point in puberty, and I'd eventually get to where he was.

The thought of this nearly broke my brittle, prepubescent brain. "I will *never* be like Sam," I said with the same conviction as Kirk Douglas and company saying, "I am Spartacus."

"Okay, honey. Okay," Mama Zane replied.

For two years, I avoided Sam like he was gonorrhea, which is to say I did my best to avoid him, but he'd still manage to find me. He had no idea that I was doing this. He had no clue that for two years, I continuously asked Adam, our mutual best friend, if Sam was "cured."

Yes, "cured" was the word I used, as if he had an affliction of being attracted to hot blondes with big fake breasts—an affliction that plagues 95 percent of straight and bisexual men.

Adam, trying to keep the peace, always said, "Yes, don't worry. He's not a pervert. He doesn't do that anymore." It was a lie, but what else was poor Adam to say, stuck in the crossfire between his two best friends?

By seventh grade, porn was all the rage. Every kid in my class watched it, and people were not shy to discuss their diets. So, it grew more and more challenging to avoid watching and discussing it. Besides, I wanted to keep my friends. If I wrote off every boy watching porn at thirteen, I'd be one lonely middle schooler.

Seeking guidance, I spoke to my two older brothers, asking if they watched porn.

"Yes," they said in unison before I could finish my question.

When I voiced my objections to porn, Niko called me out. "*Why* is it bad?" he asked. Somehow, no one had ever asked me that question. I had no actual response to *why* it was bad besides "It just is."

Niko then went on to explain that porn isn't bad. Sex isn't bad. Nudity isn't bad. It's all a natural part of life. It's also fun and something I should explore. I really looked up to both my older brothers growing up (and still do). With their permission granted, I decided I would watch porn.

"Hold on," Niko said. "Let me give you some magazines. The internet is insane, and I don't think you can handle it," he said. He was right. There was zero chance I could handle what was on the interwebs if I couldn't even stomach eBaum's World.

Niko had a stash of magazines from his best friend, who had lifted them from his dad. I first opened *Hustler*, and even that was too much to handle. I was horrified by the model's monster cock, three times the size of mine. It was just so big. And when he put it inside of her . . .

That was how sex looked? I don't know what I thought sex looked like, but this seemed so *aggressive*. Her face was either displaying pain or pleasure—maybe both.* I quickly abandoned *Hustler* and opened up *Lesbian Licks*. Without the big, hunky man with a dick the size of my forearm, I felt comfortable enough to start stroking.

For six months between seventh and eighth grade, I tried masturbating nearly every night, but I never came. I spoke to my friends about it constantly. What was I doing wrong? They tried to coach me, but how do you coach someone to masturbate at that age, or any age? "Grip your dick and stroke it up and down. If something feels good, keep doing it." Sounds simple enough, but you'd be surprised.

My inability to cum became the talk of the town. (All right, I'm not sure how true that was but at least all my friends knew about it.) And boy, did I feel like *shit* when, in seventh grade, we were at a Shabbaton (a sleepover trip my Jewish school did) and every guy was in their bunk jacking off. We were silent, but the moment we came, we'd say, "Finished." I was the last of eight guys to cum, and eventually, a friend of mine said, "Zach, if it hasn't happened by now, it's not going to happen."

To be the only guy who couldn't shoot a load? That did not make me feel good—not one bit. At least my friends weren't assholes about it. In hindsight, they probably weren't as consumed with my inability to orgasm as I was.

Then, one night, it happened. I was on my waterbed looking at *Lesbian Licks*, and I felt a little ember. I grabbed one tissue to ejaculate into, but that was not nearly enough. It was like in those old cartoons where Daffy Duck would try to put out a fire, but the moment the water shot out of the fire hose, he started flying everywhere. After ejaculat-

---

*In hindsight, I was probably also attracted to the daddy with washboard abs and a horse cock, but I was in no place to process that.

ing for what felt like an eternity, I felt like I had just run a marathon. I relaxed in bed with the biggest smile on my face. Finally, I had done it. I had fucking cum!

The next day, I told Sam. (Since I'd given up my anti-porn crusade, we were friends again.) He still makes an impression of how I told him. "It was *everywhere*," he says with big, bulbous eyes.

It wasn't long after that when I decided I was ready for internet porn. Porn then was as it is now: a lot of that *rough* shit. I fell down that rabbit hole fast. Within a week, I was watching the most brutal gangbangs and roughest throatfucking you could imagine. I was watching women get choked to the point of nearly passing out. I saw women take humongous boners so far down their throats you could see the dicks bulging through their esophagi. It was the type of porn where you immediately shut your laptop the moment after your climax.

Now I bring up those three types of sex because I still love them. Rough gangbangs? Fuck me up. Choking? Air is overrated. Throatfucking? Don't let me breathe. But I should not have been first exposed to that when I was thirteen, or at least not without proper education from sex educators explaining what porn is: a fantasy. While the emerging genres of feminist porn and ethical porn tend to be more "real," mainstream porn doesn't depict "real" sex one bit.

Still, it's okay that most porn is a fantasy—it's actually a great thing. Porn offers an opportunity for our desires to run free without judgment, shame, or fear. But that is also a dangerous prospect, not because we shouldn't have freedom in our sexual imagination—get weird, my dudes and dudettes—but because these imaginations often come into stark, disappointing contrast with reality.

Therein lies the issue. We need to understand that porn is not sex and sex is not porn. It's like comparing apples to dildos. Not to mention that all too often, fantasies are just that: fantasies. Do I actually want a masked man to break into my apartment, pin me down, tie me up, and forcefully have his way with me? No, that sounds like a traumatic experience that would cause severe psychological damage for the rest of my life. But do I get turned on by consensual non-consensual porn? Yes, something about the idea of a stronger man overtaking and ravishing me turns me on. Sue me!

But at thirteen, I didn't know how to unpack that. Going out on a limb here, but I'm going to assume *no* child can unpack that. And Lord knows the first time you have sex with someone, you shouldn't slap their ass raw and call them a "dumb little whore." Though if you meet me now, you *better* do that.

X X X

As the sex columnist at *Men's Health*, I'm constantly asked about porn. Men seek counsel or absolution for their porn habits, and their partners worry that their husbands or boyfriends or whoever are full-blown addicts.

This raises a question: Is porn addiction real? There's currently a heated debate in the medical community about this. While I'm no doctor—though I watch a ton of doctor/patient porn—my take is that people, even experts, are willfully and purposefully misinterpreting this question.

Many experts state that porn addiction isn't real because "addiction" indicates something specific biologically, and porn "addiction" doesn't meet that criteria. Fair enough, but I'd argue that porn can lead to compulsive behaviors that negatively impact our lives, which ostensibly look and act like a behavioral addiction.

I've heard stories from men who cannot function unless they watch porn and claim that they cannot stop watching it. They get fired from work for viewing videos in their office. They're perpetually late to events because they're jacking off to porn. They end up divorced because they have no desire to have sex with their wives. Is it that outrageous to suggest that if porn is having a negative impact on your life and you cannot stop watching it, then yes, you have a problem, even if it doesn't technically qualify as an addiction?

Liberals, progressives, therapists, and researchers are *very* reluctant to admit that porn can cause any problem whatsoever because they know conservatives and religious zealots will take this admission and use it to further their anti-porn agenda, which is just a thinly veiled movement intended to further sexual repression, suppress women's autonomy, and vilify queers. The anti-porn crusaders will undoubtedly tell men they have a porn addiction when they do not. They'll moralize an issue that has nothing to do with your ethics as a person.

However, and I cannot overstate this, of all the men who've written in with worries about their alleged porn addiction, it's likely only a teeny-tiny handful who have had serious issues with their viewing habits. Most simply thought they were "addicted" because they have internalized sexual shame from, well, pick your poison. These men—the *vast* majority of men—don't have problems with their porn use. They're just enjoying the easy access to pleasure, fantasy, and novelty.

I think there's a world in which we can acknowledge all the incredible things about porn—it allows you to explore fantasies safely, you learn about your own desires, watching it with your partner is a great way to bond—while also recognizing that it can be damaging. And while many men are *not* technically addicted, still, it would behoove them to analyze their relationship with porn to see when it's serving them and when it's not.

For a long time, I assumed that you must build up some arousal tolerance when you watch a lot of porn. I figured that Millennials, being the first generation to grow up with unlimited access to internet porn, must struggle with erectile dysfunction, inability to orgasm, and having fulfilling sexual experiences because of their porn use. I thought this for one simple reason: I struggled with my porn use.

I used to be unable to cum unless I closed my eyes and imagined some really intense porn. Sometimes I couldn't even get hard unless I imagined rough porn. I'd have a casual hookup, be unable to cum, and the moment they left, I'd fire up the laptop and cum in twenty seconds watching videos.

So, I thought I was "addicted" to porn. But I wasn't. Rather, I was anxious about having sex with another *real* person. This was independent of porn, but I assumed porn was at the root of the issue.

I don't want to project my relationship with porn onto you, so I'll share some words from one of the top porn experts and researchers working today: Silva Neves, author of the 2021 book *Compulsive Sexual Behaviours: A Psycho-Sexual Treatment Guide for Clinicians*. "Basically, scientifically, we have not seen any brain changes with porn consumption despite what the anti-porn people say," he told me. "Most people mistake desensitization and tolerance with what actually happens: dissociation and novelty-seeking."

Now, dissociation is not a disorder. It's something we all do in other aspects of our lives. When we don't eat mindfully, we don't taste our delicious food. When we're not attempting to connect with our partner because we're checked out, we're not going to be able to get hard during sex. Then, of course, variety is the spice of life. There's nothing pathological about wanting novel sexual experiences. While your partner might not want or be able to provide you with novel sexual experiences, porn can. There is always something new, exciting, and batshit-crazy online. (I fucking *love* all the batshit-crazy vids.)

Neves continued, "PIED (porn-induced erectile dysfunction) has been largely disproved because there is not enough evidence that porn actually induces ED, but it might encourage it in various ways, i.e., unrealistic expectations of penis size, for example, which is, in my opinion, more of a poor sex education problem than a porn problem."

Let's go ahead and focus here on his last sentence because that is where it gets juicy. The issue, nearly all the time, is not porn. It's the fact that we don't have proper sex education. In school, we're lucky if we were taught anything beyond the locations of the vas deferens and fallopian tubes. We're not taught any useful information that's actually helpful when it comes to having sex! We're not taught to be mindful of our bodies and desires during sex. We're not taught enthusiastic consent, so we feel uncomfortable and sometimes even scared when we're having sex. And we *definitely* aren't taught how to talk about sex with our partners. Yet, somehow, we're supposed to know how to have pleasurable and fulfilling sex.

We also don't teach some of the more basic techniques necessary for having pleasurable sex. Notice how I don't say "great sex." That's because great sex is subjective. For example, while I, personally, don't love a dry hand job with calloused hands, that may be your thing. More power to you.

Still, there are some sexual techniques and tools that *most* people find pleasurable that would be helpful to learn. For example, using lube—and without shame! Some guys feel like they've "failed" if they can't get a woman to WAP status on their own. Some women are embarrassed to ask for lube for the same reason.*

How fabulous would it be if we encouraged the use of lube and explained the differences between the types of lube? How great would it be if we taught men where the clitoris and prostate are and how to stimulate them? Or imagine if we taught how to douche! You can change your life without having to change your sheets.

---

*I actually once had a woman yell at me when I went to grab lube. "I'm wet enough. I don't need that!" she said defensively.

There is simply so much we can teach youth *and* adults regarding pleasurable sex and communication. Each and every one of us needs this information because sex is not intuitive. It's difficult! Being naked and vulnerable in front of someone is difficult. Connecting with a partner is difficult. Being a throat goat is difficult. Having sex can induce any number of anxieties—about your body, desires, and attractions. Any number of these factors seem a more likely cause for not being able to orgasm than an unflinching porn addiction.

All right, since I keep belaboring how porn isn't the same as real sex, and we need more proper sex education, allow me to explain. Porn would have you believe that the average dick size is nine inches. All sex is rough sex. Sex is over once a man cums. All women can squirt buckets across the room. All men shoot thick, viscous loads. Nonbinary people don't exist. You should make loud, exaggerated moans while you're doing it. Women (and bottoms) love to be jackhammered to smithereens. You should last for thirty minutes, maybe even an hour. No one uses condoms. No one uses lube. No one farts. No one queefs. No one has trouble orgasming. No one has trouble staying hard. No one asks for consent, or even discusses what they like or don't like. Your father isn't properly satisfying your stepmom, so if she catches you jacking off, she will tell you you're doing it all wrong and give you the best head you've ever had in your life.

Excluding my final point, these things are wrong!

Still, this doesn't mean porn is "bad." However, porn without proper sexual health information *is* bad. If you're anti-porn, you should be *pro* sex education. But anti-porn crusaders are not because porn is just a wedge issue used for a larger, more nebulous purpose: to promote sex-negativity and instill shame as a means of control.

In case you're wondering, I still watch a fair amount of porn, though these days my consumption ebbs and flows. Now, however, when I'm struggling to cum with a sexual partner, which still happens periodically (it's normal!), I don't shut my eyes and log onto the World Wide Web. I kiss them harder. I thrust deeper and make even more eye contact. I try to connect with them and get aroused by the flesh-and-blood hottie in front of me, instead of fantasizing about someone I've never met.

And if that doesn't get me to cum, I tell them to sit on my face while they deepthroat me. That always does the trick.

PART II

SEXUAL CONFUSION

CHAPTER 3

WHERE'S MY LIGHTBULB MOMENT?

When I was sixteen, I had long, dirty blond hair that approached my nipples and a set of bulky braces that could be seen from space when I smiled. I couldn't grow a beard just yet, but I could sing my heart out, which was why I was cast as the dentist in my high school production of *Little Shop of Horrors*.

I was madly in love with my then-girlfriend, but I was also gay—or, at least so thought the musical director. One evening after rehearsal, he called me over and said he'd like to discuss my "movements." I was a little confused because the dentist didn't have particularly tough movements. It wasn't like I was playing SpongeBob on Broadway.*

While discussing my "movements," he couldn't look me in the eyes as he said, "So, um . . . I just want to say that I support you and how you live your life out of the theater."

That's a weird thing to say, I thought.

He continued, "But onstage, it's important to really act as the character, and I don't think the dentist would walk the way you do. His gait would be firmer, and his wrists would be . . . less bent."

At the wrist comment, I picked up what he was putting down. While queers weren't as visible back in 2008, we still had Neil Patrick Harris, Ellen DeGeneres, and *The Rocky Horror Picture Show*, which I'd seen a few midnight screenings of. So I knew what having limp wrists meant. I said I understood, mostly to put our painfully awkward conversation to an end.

---

*Ethan Slater should have won that damn Tony!

My girlfriend was waiting by the door and asked, "What was that about?"

"Oh, he thinks I'm gay."

She laughed. "Yeah, what's new?"

X X X

Since I was a young kid, there were rumors about me being gay. And you know what? I get it. I *was* a little fucking faggot. (I'M ALLOWED TO SAY THIS, YOU CAN'T. UNLESS YOU'RE QUEER. THEN YOU CAN.)

I mean, look at me:

I embodied countless gay stereotypes. I was a sensitive boy with limp wrists and a love of musical theater. But my voice would also jump four octaves when I got excited, and I excelled in water polo—the gayest sport of all time.* The clincher: I got furious when anyone used "gay" as a slur. Mind you, this was in the early 2000s—everyone was using gay pejoratively. Still, brave, little, exceptionally straight Zach, with his Hawaiian shirt and umbrella in ear, would passionately call out everyone who used the word "gay" as a slur. Luckily, I had the excuse of my uncle to justify my protest without arousing suspicion. I would always shout, "Don't say that! My uncle is gay!"

I really did not think *I* was queer! While I knew I was a little different, I was in deep denial. I thought I was one of those creative straights—a John Mulaney type. Yet, I hung a giant poster of Aquaman above my bed when I was thirteen that remained until after I graduated college. This was well before Jason Momoa starred in the blockbuster film, and the poster that hung above my bed was *far* gayer than any mainstream movie would ever allow for.

Aquaman stood contrapposto, posing on a mountain of treasure with a pirate ship behind him. It takes a moment to realize that there's a sunken ship; at first, you're far too distracted looking at his abs. Shirtless, he has a twelve-pack—maybe even an eighteen-pack. I'm pretty sure the illustrator created new muscles to make him look impossibly ripped. Once you finally look up, you notice his long, blond locks floating effortlessly in the ocean. Aquaman's smolder was *almost* angry, and you could see his cut jawline through his blond beard.

And his massive bulge . . . It was prominently displayed smack dab in the middle of the poster. I like to think his bulge was watching over me at night, keeping me safe—a homoerotic dream catcher of sorts.

Still, I insisted I was straight because one thing was for certain: I loved women, and not in a gay BFF, "I love my girl besties!" kind of way. I mean I wanted to nail some chicks, bro.

So I focused my attractions on women throughout high school. That

---

*It's just half-naked men groping each other's muscles underwater.

wasn't incredibly difficult because I was indeed attracted to them. That's the beautiful thing about bisexuality—I could be obsessed with boobs and still sleep under Aquaman, though I think Aquaman's enormous pecs may qualify as boobs.

I think that if I was gay, I would have been forced to come to terms with my sexuality sooner. It's not that it was less "urgent" because I was bisexual; rather, my attractions to women weren't a lie. Each time I spoke about how "hot" I found a girl, I wasn't pushing myself deeper into the closet. I could genuinely participate in conversations with boys about which girls we found attractive. And it wasn't like my girlfriend was a beard. I loved her, and those feelings were real.

So throughout my teenage years, I compartmentalized—there was the men box and the women box. In middle and high school, I only took the women box off the shelf. Still, as though possessed by a demon from a horror film, the men box would occasionally fly off the shelf without my touching it. The only way to put that box back on the shelf? Rationalize and deny, baby!

Whenever I looked longingly at a man's dick while watching straight porn, I'd tell myself, "That's not gay! You have to look at his dick, otherwise you can't see any penetration." I also gravitated toward categories of porn that were deemed straight but were still very homoerotic, like gangbangs—a fabulous loophole wherein heterosexual sex just so happens to feature fifteen naked dudes with nice cocks. Often, these men would try to stay hard, so they'd be jerking off in the background. Hot! And if their dicks accidentally touched? Chef's kiss. But hey, there was female supervision. I could cum my face off to a bunch of dudes and still be 100 percent straight!

Even though I could teach a master class in compartmentalization, there were still times when I simply could not help but question. The years of rumors behind my back—and being called gay right to my face—gave me pause. Maybe everyone was onto something. After all, I didn't know any other straight boy who had a three-foot-tall Aquaman poster in his room. And my eyes did linger a little bit longer on good-looking men. Even this I managed to rationalize. Instead of admitting that I had a sexual attraction to men, I prided myself in being comfortable enough with my masculinity to acknowledge when a man was hot. But no matter what I told myself, I still knew I was not looking respectfully.

Eventually, the intrusive thoughts and desires became too much to bear, so my second week of college, I purposefully took the man box off the shelf for the first time. By that I mean I decided that I was going to hook up with a dude. I didn't tell anyone, had no idea who the lucky winner would be, but figured college was the time to explore. That was what everyone seemed to say. There was the added benefit that my closest friends and family were three thousand miles away, back in California—a deliberate choice. In distance, there was a sense of anonymity and safety; I did not want anyone in my hometown to know about my sexual exploits. If word got out that I hooked up with a man, everyone would label me as gay—even if my explorations led to the conclusion that I was indeed straight.

In the second week of my freshman year, I found him. He had light-green eyes and curly black hair with a scruffy little beard to match. He was both a rugby player and a gymnast, all abs and ass, and I was smitten.

Typically, I'm the loudest person in the room, but at this house party, he put me to shame. We kept shouting over each other, neither of us listening to what the other had to say, but it hardly mattered. In between talking about Lord knows what, we would take a shot. Then another one. Then about nine more. I needed more than a little liquid courage if I was going to go home with a man.

Back in his dorm room we began messily sloshing tongues, and I felt a stray beard hair land in my mouth. There was no denying it—I was definitely making out with a man. He took off my underwear and I took off his. While looking down at his dick, a huge smile crept over my face.

"No, you're not huge. I'm just really small," he said as if reading my mind.

"Damn it, really?"

"Yeah . . . I mean your dick is great, but it's not big." Before I could reply he pushed me back on his bed, got on his knees, and began sucking. He took my whole dick in his mouth like a champion. Never had a woman deepthroated me like him. He made it look easy. To him, it was easy.

Suddenly I felt my throat swell. I quickly excused myself and sprinted to the bathroom, where I proceeded to vomit. When I thought I had gotten the last chunks out of my system, I headed back to his room. He asked if I was okay, and I said that I just needed to pee. I then threw off my undies and he began sucking again, but nope—I was not done. I rushed to the bathroom again to puke a second time.

"Are you sure you're okay?" he asked when I returned.

"Yeah, I'm totally fine," I said. "Just a little drunk. Let's head to bed."

All things considered, the next morning wasn't that awkward, likely due to his vast experience hooking up with straight-identifying men. (Later, I'd come to learn that "turning guys" was kinda his whole thing.) We both acknowledged it was a "crazy night," I said I'd see him around, and I left.

I spent the rest of that Saturday feeling like I got hit by that same bus that took out Regina George. I was too hungover to analyze or process that I had hooked up with a guy. But come Sunday, I was in crisis mode. *Did this make me gay? Did I actually enjoy it? Does the experience even "count"? I was so drunk.*

I thought I was going to have a moment of clarity—a lightbulb moment—when I kissed another man. The second my lips touched his, I would know, *definitively*, if I was gay or straight. Either I would love the touch of a man—feeling his mouth against mine would unlock something essential about desire and passion and make my experiences with women pale in comparison—or I'd be grossed out. Frankly, at that point, I didn't care whether I was gay or straight. I just wanted clarity.

Alas, I didn't have a polarizing response, and that's when I started to spiral. *I got hard, so clearly that meant something, right? If I wasn't into it, then I wouldn't have been able to get erect. But I am also eighteen, and the sight of a particularly plump tomato is enough to make me hard, so having his lips around my dick? Obviously that's going to make me pop a boner. I didn't mind kissing him, but that beard hair—I did not like that, so maybe I'm not gay?*

I decided to do some recon. I asked a few gay friends at what point they knew they were gay and what their first same-sex experience was like. Their experiences were definitive: When they kissed a man, they *knew*. That decided it. I was not gay. I loved and enjoyed having sex with women, so I simply could not be gay.

Why, then, did I spend the next four years of my life waking up naked and hungover in other men's beds? Why had I kept busting in their mouths, and how come I had rug burn on my cheeks from kissing men with five o'clock shadows? It all seemed pretty fucking gay.

While I did my best to not think about it—and to explore without feeling compelled to pick a label—I couldn't completely gloss over my behaviors. Maybe if it was once in a blue moon, I could have gotten away without analyzing, but by the end of college, hooking up with guys had become a frequent pastime. Countless mornings, I woke up to find that I had drunkenly jacked off to gay porn the night before. Many nights I went to bed contemplating my sexuality.

It's wild to me how these thoughts were at the forefront of my mind while simultaneously not being salient. The brain truly is a miraculous organ. I was obsessed with figuring out my sexual identity while pretending that I wasn't. No matter how much I told myself that I was okay without having my sexual identity figured out, I still felt alone. I was anxious. I was convinced there was no one else in the world like me.

If this all sounds confusing, it's because it was very fucking confusing.

Now, here is where even I am impressed by my mental gymnastics. By the time I graduated from college I had gotten blown by a dozen guys, made out with at least thirty dudes, and even fucked one fella in the ass (on two separate occasions), but I still believed I was straight. This was because I had done all of the above—and much more—with even more *women* in that same amount of time.

When talk of my *extremely gay* sexual exploits made it around campus, people naturally asked if I was, in fact, gay.* "Nope, but a mouth is a mouth," I would reply, or "Drunk Zach is another man I do not know. You'll have to ask him." Getting sloshed also helped with my cognitive dissonance. I could always blame it on the a-a-a-a-a-a-alcohol. *I would never hook up with a guy sober*, I told myself, as if that made it any less gay.

At this point you might be thinking, "Zach, you clearly seem bisexual—how did you not know?" To this I reply, "I am old."

There was very little bisexual visibility back then. I maybe knew one out bi person—a woman—who we all thought was doing it for attention.† I didn't know a single out bi man. And while my personal life lacked a bounty of bisexuals, there weren't exactly bisexuals busting at the seams of Hollywood either. There weren't even any bisexual stereotypes. I would have killed for some stereotypes. That would have at least meant that we were real.

---

*It was a valid question, despite it being a very nosy and annoying one.
†It was 2009, and we didn't know that bi women do it for attention and *also* because they're trying to get finger-blasted by a lipstick lesbian.

Only recently has "bi culture" found stereotypes, though they mostly apply to women. If she has her hair dyed light green, wears a septum ring, hangs a crystal around her neck, and cuffs her jeans, she has definitely three-way kissed a man and woman at the same time. Sadly, to this day, there still isn't much bi culture for men, except that we dress like either lumberjacks or magicians. While accurate, as a bi man that falls into the camp of magicians, I take offense.

Even without cultural or personal touchstones, the thought did periodically cross my mind. During my sophomore year I bravely turned to the all-knowing holder of knowledge: Google. A quick search of "bisexual guy" yielded mostly academic articles about bisexual men having or spreading HIV. There were maybe a few scattered articles debating whether bisexuality is real and a "10 Things to Never Say to a Bisexual Person," but that was it. There was very limited information for someone who was still *questioning* his sexuality.*

It didn't help that my guy friends who identified as bisexual came out as "full-blown gay" shortly after. I didn't know a single man in college who claimed the bi label permanently. So I believed it was a layover, and all men who claimed to be bi were just waiting for their connecting flight.

Hopefully now it's clearer to see why I didn't think I was bisexual. How could I be the *only* man in the world with this unique sexual orientation? While I was egocentric, I wasn't delusional.

But after sleeping my way through a not insignificant chunk of the Vassar student body, I had a conversation with my eldest brother that I simply could not ignore. We were drinking margaritas at our favorite Tex-Mex restaurant, and I started sharing my sexual exploits with men and women, still describing myself as straight, when he interrupted me.

---

*A little humblebrag here, but if you Google "bisexual guy" now, you'll see that I wrote two of the top four articles.

"You know, Zach. I experimented in college with guys for a little before realizing I was straight. I think Niko even kissed a guy, too. We're all effeminate and have many gay qualities, so it makes sense that we'd experiment." He then took a deep breath. "But you have been experimenting for five years. At some point, you're no longer experimenting. At some point, you're just, ya know—"

I knew that wasn't meant as a read, but I felt dragged! There was simply no comeback, so I deflected with a joke. "Oh, God! I'm gonna end up married to a man and on our fortieth anniversary give a toast where I thank him for staying with me as I continue to explore my sexuality."

As adept as I had become at rationalizing my behaviors, I couldn't argue with logic. It had been five years and countless men. That's simply not straight. That conversation was a turning point—I needed to get my act together. I didn't want to spend the rest of my life getting blacked out to have sex with men. I was tired of spiraling every time I saw an attractive man and wanted to have a goddamn answer when someone asked me whether I was gay or straight. So I decided to see a therapist, my first one as an adult.

X X X

Unpopular opinion, but the term "visibility" infuriates me. I think it's overused and hailed as a panacea to fix the world's social problems. It doesn't help that I see classically masculine gays on Instagram claiming their thirst traps are visibility. Don't get me wrong, I love seeing your cum gutters on my feed, but what are you making visible? Being hot? The CW has been providing hot male visibility for nearly two decades. You are way behind, my friend.

Nevertheless, I believe that visibility is a form of activism. In fact, it's a necessary first stage of activism. Essentially, visibility posits: "Look, we're real! We're not this tiny group. There are a lot of us, and we want you to acknowledge our existence, and treat us with a little respect."

Of course, visibility isn't just for a majority group to recognize that a minority group exists. It's also for the minority group to learn that they are not alone. I can sum up my years of writing with one insight: I am not special. Yes, I've probably attended more sex parties than you, but my struggles with defining my identity are not unique. I have received hundreds of messages from bi folks across the globe thanking me for sharing my story. Though they hadn't met an openly bi man, many of my experiences mirrored theirs. Hearing my story—as well as my struggles—helped them realize that they're not alone.

This matters. A constant refrain from those who think of or turn to suicide is loneliness, especially among queer people. It is incredibly damaging to feel like you have no community, no one to talk to, or that you're a pariah in a straight world that discriminates, bullies, and harasses. "Being LGBTQ alone does not put a young person at higher risk for suicide; the discrimination, rejection, fear, and harassment that may come with being LGBTQ in an unsupportive environment are what increase the risk," the NYC Department of Health website states eloquently.

The numbers are still staggering, despite how far we have come. Gay and bisexual men are four times more likely to commit suicide than straight men. Today, suicide is a cause of death for more queer men than AIDS.

And don't even get me started on bi women. Bi women are nearly twice as likely as straight women to experience sexual and physical assault. Bi women also have much higher rates of drug addiction and abuse. Not to mention that lesbians are really mean to bi women. At least gay men still hang out with bi men. Yes, they'll talk shit behind our backs, about how we're in denial, but they're not as blatantly antagonistic as lesbians who make bi women feel like gender traitors for breaking up with a woman and dating a man.

And let us not forget that roughly a third of trans people identify as bisexual or pansexual. Roughly 20 percent identify as queer, which could also indicate an attraction to multiple or all genders. Whereas only roughly 15 percent of trans folks identify as straight and roughly the same number identify as gay. For a woke generation who throws the word "intersectionality" around like hotcakes, I'm shocked that I've seen no individuals or studies address the relationship between biphobia and the violence trans women face.

All right, please excuse my impassioned rant, but there *is* a point to all this: As much as I hate visibility as a buzzword, I understand how crucial it is in the beginning of any movement. And yes, bisexuals are having a goddamn movement.

But visibility poses unique challenges for bi folks. You can't be "visibly" bi. When a brand hires all dark-skin Black women or larger-bodied women for their beauty campaign, we agree it's a win for a type of visibility. While not exactly the same for trans and gay representation, as you can't necessarily tell if someone is trans or gay by looking at them, there are clear visual iconographies for trans and gay culture (rainbow flag, a twink with bleached-blond tips, etc.). Now, say GLAAD wanted to partner with Dove for a bi visibility campaign—how would that work? There would have to be a little PSA that says, "By the way, they're all bisexual!"

Then there's the issue of bi relationships being categorically undefinable. A man dating another man is colloquially in a "gay relationship" whereas a man dating a woman is in a "straight relationship." Really the only way for a relationship to "read" as bi would be if you're polyamorous and have both a boyfriend and a girlfriend. While that sounds like paradise to me, the vast majority of bi people aren't looking to be in a mixed-gender throuple.* Since, colloquially, you can't be in a dyadic bisexual relationship—rather, you are a bisexual person in a gay or straight relationship with another person—it's harder to remember, let alone see, there are bisexuals among us.

Bisexual people are only visibly bisexual when we announce our sexuality. Really, bisexual visibility is a misnomer; we should say bisexual audibility. If I wasn't constantly shouting about my bisexuality from the rooftops—which I have made a career out of—I'd be labeled as gay. Actually, I'm still labeled as gay by many, despite being (in)famously bisexual.

Declaring our bisexuality is a pain in the ass, but it's a necessary chore. It's why we must claim bisexuality even when we're happily monogamous and have been married to the same person for years. It's why we claim bisexuality even if we've never had sex with someone of the same or different gender. It's why we say it loud and proud all the time.

And if someone doesn't believe you, do you know what's more effective than trying to convince them? Letting them know you don't have to. When you tell someone "That's okay, I'm secure in my sexuality and don't need your validation," you'll quickly see them backpedal. This is to say, you don't have to spend your life in constant debates with others about your identity. You can if you want to, but it's exhausting. You can simply express that you're bi and move right along!

The best part about being bi is learning that bi people are literally *everywhere.* There's this saying, "If you want to find a gay man, go to a gay bar. If you want to find a bisexual, go to the grocery store." The moment you say you're bi, folks feel confident sharing that they're bi, too—that's bisexual audibility in action, baby! In my experience, folks

---

*But if you are, please slide into my DMs.

might not be as comfortable uttering the word, but they will share that they've had partners of various genders, or like sleeping with both men and women, or have been questioning their sexuality. This happens often because most bi people are starved to talk about being bi. While they're not necessarily closeted *per se*, they only share their sexuality once they've confirmed they're talking to another bi person. Otherwise, they don't correct when someone wrongly assumes that they're either gay or straight. It's a mitzvah to give these people the opportunity to discuss an element of their identity that is so salient yet seldom acknowledged.

Now, over a decade after I first Googled "bisexual guy," I am surrounded by bi people. Most of my friends are bi. Most of my partners are bi. Most of my community is bi. I went from not knowing a single openly bi person to being inundated. I went from thinking we don't exist to thinking that we're most of the population. If nineteen-year-old Zach could see me now, he'd be shooketh by the brazenly bisexual babe he'd become. He'd be shocked to see his openly bisexual family who love and support one another.

If only I knew that the answer was more bisexual audibility. I wouldn't have spent countless nights so preoccupied that I couldn't sleep. I wouldn't have had to get sloshed to be intimate with a man. I wouldn't have had to live with the weight of rationalizing my cognitive dissonance. I wouldn't have felt shame for my behaviors. I would have simply embraced being bisexual and found my bi community a hell of a lot sooner.

CHAPTER 4

COCAINE TURNED ME BISEXUAL

By the end of college, I knew that I desperately needed to have penetrative sex with a man, but I was afraid to admit that desperate desire. The desire existed *right* below the threshold of consciousness, yet this latent need seemingly guided my actions for the past four years. It's why I woke up in the beds of countless men, naked and hungover, unsure of how I got there or what we did. It's why I took multiple queer theory courses. It's why I relished playing spin the bottle with my a cappella group. It gave me carte blanche to make out with guys without it being gay.* And it's why I ended up at the apartment of my friend Jackson, who had told my past girlfriend, while we were monogamous, "I'm going to fuck your boyfriend if it's the last thing I do."

So, there I was at seven thirty on my last Wednesday night before graduation, watching Jackson cook a rotisserie chicken in his tiny apartment. To give you a sense of its size, I felt claustrophobic when I walked in, and I'm someone who prefers pooping in the smaller stalls, but this—this was a lot even for me.

Jackson, who is now a beefy gay porn star with an ass that launched a thousand ships, was then just Jack, a twinky aspiring composer with an ass that launched a mere five hundred ships. Jack was very handsome but not intimidatingly so. I could look and talk to him without getting too distracted. He was also confident, consistently getting men to sleep with him, without being aggressive. That finesse was key since I wasn't going to make the first move.

---

*It was still pretty fucking gay.

After a few minutes at his place, Jack began cutting lines of cocaine on his little kitchen countertop in between checking the temperature of the chicken with a thermometer.

I had managed to make it to my senior year without trying coke, which wasn't a simple feat. While I'd been offered on repeated occasions, I always politely declined. Cocaine was one of my no-no drugs, whereas marijuana, shrooms, acid, and drinking two Four Lokos were totally chill.

But like on Passover, this night was different from all other nights. So when Jack offered, I paused before responding with absolutely zero conviction, "I better not." He sensed my false decline, so when he insisted, I not so reluctantly acquiesced. It was my last week of college, and a general sentiment of YOLO was in the air. Everyone was desperately trying to do all the things and people they hadn't yet.

I was hoping cocaine would give me a heightened version of liquid courage. I knew it boosted confidence and lowered inhibitions, which was exactly what I needed to have sex with a man. Even though I was *definitely* only there to eat his chicken and not his cake.

After snorting a fat line, I felt like every bone in my body was going to jump out and dance a 1920s jig. I was flooded with fleeting thoughts but couldn't focus on one.

Come nine forty-five, the chicken was not ready, and I had not stuck my penis into Jack's butt. I hadn't even kissed him. I was hoping—though totally not hoping—that something sexual would have happened by now. Alas, I had to attend rehearsal for my a cappella group, of which I was the president. Yes, I was the head of my a cappella group at Vassar College and somehow thought I was straight. Jack said I should come back after, and this was when I actually gave a hard no.

"Zach, you haven't even tried my chicken yet, and there's no way you're going to sleep with how much coke you did. Just come back over," he said. I couldn't argue with his logic.

The next hour and a half dragged. I kept checking my phone every four minutes to see if rehearsal was over. My legs couldn't stop shaking, and everyone was speaking at a glacial pace. At exactly eleven thirty, I dismissed them and ran back to Jack's apartment.

He wasn't in his loungewear like last time. He was wearing a semi-translucent button-down shirt and a pair of tight black jeans revealing his perfectly sculpted bubble butt. (Okay, 750 ships!) Arsema, his roommate who slept on the twin bed next to his, was there and also dressed to the nines.

Arsema was one of my best friends. There was never any sexual tension between us because she identified as asexual. Knowing that she had no interest in sex, I quickly got over how attractive I found her because she was stunning. Still, even when we were naked or half-naked, our interactions were always platonic. Once, our mutual friend walked into her dorm room to find the two of us lying on her bed. I was shirtless, and Arsema was brushing my chest hair with a comb. "You guys are so weird," she said. "Make sure you clean out my brush before you put it back." That was the type of strange, intimate friendship we had.

"Why are you guys dressed up?" I asked them.

"We're going out to a gay club," Jack said as if the answer was obvious.

There were no clubs in Poughkeepsie, and there definitely weren't any gay clubs. "I'm sorry, what?"

"Yeah, my friend is this big New York City drag queen, and we can get in for free and get bottle service."

This sounded incredibly suspect. It was a random Wednesday night in Poughkeepsie. *Why on Earth would an NYC drag queen be upstate hosting a party? And bottle service? What?*

Confused, I turned to Arsema. "Are you going out?"

"*Yup*, and if I'm doing this shit, you are, too," she replied.

Whether it was peer pressure, cocaine, or the fact that I didn't but also really did want to have sex with Jack, I found myself going to a gay club in Poughkeepsie on a Wednesday night. I did so despite knowing that my seminar grade depended on not vomiting during my presentation the next day.

Since I wasn't wearing appropriate clubbing attire, Jack said I could borrow one of his shirts, which I'm going to go ahead and simply describe as gay. A fifteen-minute Uber ride later, and lo and behold, there was a massive club in an area of Poughkeepsie I had never explored, which, to be fair, was the vast majority of Poughkeepsie. (I was too busy exploring the student body, am I right, ladies?)* Inside, there were a total of five people sitting around a table, drinking vodka sodas. After Jack introduced us to the drag queen, we spent the next two hours pounding vodka soda after vodka soda until we ditched the soda and went for straight shots, taking conspicuous key bumps between rounds.

Since drunk Zach had a thing for men, it didn't take long until Jack and I were hardcore smooching. My hands freely roamed his body but always made their way back to his ass. (Fine, nine hundred ships!) Touching those plump cheeks made my dick involuntarily pulse and rub my zipper, which only made me harder.

By the time we left, Jack, Arsema, and I were past wasted. Still, Arsema knew to give Jack and me some alone time back at the apartment. We opened the door and fell onto the mattress—our limbs entangled as we gave each other wet, open-mouth kisses. Then he slid off his skinny jeans, revealing his bare ass. The sight of his jockstrap nearly sobered me up. I didn't know then how ubiquitous jockstraps were in the gay community. I thought it was this wild thing that only a handful

---

*Kill me now.

of really kinky guys were into. Seeing it confirmed what I was about to do: fuck a dude in the butt.

It had been nearly four years since I first got my dick sucked, and countless men had sucked it since, but this was different. I knew that some straight guys fuck around with dudes and get blown, but if I was having anal sex with a man, there was no turning back. This final booty-ful frontier was all-caps GAY. I would have to stretch a hell of a lot more for my mental gymnastics after this.

Luckily, before I could process my fear, Jack grabbed my dick with a handful of lube and thrust me into his behind. My worries vanished instantly inside his tight hole. All I could think about was how slippery he felt and how much of my dick he could take. And his booty was so smooth; it was like a lady butt! (A thousand fucking ships! Are you happy? His ass was as good back then as it is now.) Still, I didn't close my eyes and pretend he was a woman. No, I kissed and fucked him without breaking eye contact, and I loved every goddamn minute of it.

Clarity washed over me: This was what I wanted—what I'd always wanted. Rock hard, I pounded and pounded. Then, I noticed a hazy red light in front of me. I thought the coke was making me hallucinate, but when I turned around, I saw Arsema, completely naked, standing on a chair. I hadn't heard her come in or get undressed, so you could only imagine my shock when I saw that in one hand, she held up a red "mood" light, and with her other hand, she was filming us on her iPhone.

My brain simply could not process what she was doing, so I went back to fucking Jack. I didn't say a word, and neither did she. When I changed Jack to yet another position, I realized he was done. He was fucked, satisfied, and needed to pass out.

So I turned to Arsema. She got down from her chair.

I was still hard, and Arsema stared directly at my dick. "You make all these jokes about having a small dick, but it's not small," she said.

Like a putz, I replied, "Do you want to touch it?"

Given the fact she'd identified as asexual for as long as I'd known her, I did not expect her to grab my dick and say, "Fuck me."

We fucked for two hours or ten minutes. All I know is the sun was rising by the time we finished. "Can I cum in you?" I asked on the verge of busting.

"Not unless you want children," she replied.

Exhausted but still wired, we both lay on that tiny twin mattress with Jack beside us. After catching our breath, we turned to each other and at the same time said, "Food?" It was seven thirty in the morning. I quickly emailed my vocal coach to say I had food poisoning and couldn't attend rehearsal, and then we walked to the corner with four fast-food restaurants and bought our favorite item from each. When we finished, I headed back to my apartment, showered, changed, and went directly to give my two-hour presentation on the cognitive science and neurophysiology of gut feelings. Somehow, I still managed to get an A in that class.

X X X

Cocaine will always hold a special place in my heart because it gave me the confidence to explore my sexuality. (A weird win for cocaine, I'm aware.) But before cocaine, it was alcohol and cannabis. Over the course of five years, I'd hooked up with several men, and I was always *very* fucked-up—like can't-walk-in-a-straight-line fucked-up.

Of course, I'm not the only queer man who has required drugs or alcohol to be sexually intimate with men. Many closeted men need liquid or powdered courage to act on their feelings. Many out men do, too. I know guys who can only have sex with other dudes when they're drunk, and they have been out as gay for years.

It's not an accident queer men have significantly higher rates of drug and alcohol use than straight men. It's not that we party more than straight guys—though some of us definitely do. It's that many queer men cannot embrace same-sex intimacy sober. Often, shame is the cause. In my case, it was a combination of uncertainty and fear (with, of course, a little bit of shame sprinkled in). I didn't know what I wanted, or at least not consciously, but when I was fucked-up, I could just act without thinking.

Then, while I logically knew that there wasn't anything shameful about being queer, I think I also knew, deep down, that once I embraced being queer, my life would change forever. My politics, my community, my everything would be different. For two decades, I thought I was a cis, white straight dude and, as such, lived a privileged life. Thinking about the struggles of being part of a marginalized community was scary. You know what helped me not think about or feel this pressure? Drugs and alcohol! Shove that shit up my nose, damn it. Put my big schnoz to use!

While I had a moment of sobriety amidst fucking Jack when I admitted to having an attraction to men—looking him in the eyes and allowing myself to enjoy the experience—I was back to my mental gymnastics the next day. Somehow, I managed to get even more limber.

This time the blame was on cocaine. Drugs and alcohol were my get-out-of-gay-jail-free card that I kept using over and over again. You better believe I used it with Jack, too. Somehow, no one had ever called me out on my bullshit. No one said, "If you like doing this drunk, you probably like doing this sober." I doubt I would have been receptive to hearing that, but I'm still surprised no one ever said it.

By the time I was twenty-one, I had spent four years surrounded by queer men, women, and nonbinary folks at Vassar. I didn't think being gay was wrong; in hindsight, I've realized it was my aversion to ambiguity—not knowing who I was attracted to—that was holding me back. I've always craved clarity. So saying out loud, "I am confused with my sexuality, and I don't know who I'm genuinely attracted to," was not an option. My OCD brain simply could not handle that level of uncertainty.

There was also a part of me that knew that "confused" or "questioning" was synonymous with "gay and in denial."

"Questioning" is a part of the larger LGBTQQIP2SAA acronym.* The fact that "questioning" is the second Q in the expanded alphabet soup proves my point. The queer gods responsible for adding new letters were like, "Yeah, the questioning guys are definitely faggots, so let's throw 'em in preemptively."

I do not believe that questioning your sexuality automatically makes you a member of the LGBTQ community. We all question some element of our sexuality. I've had friends who questioned and realized, nope, they're straight. They're just a little more creative, effeminate, and love drag—attributes that can exist alongside heterosexuality. I love those friends deeply, but they are not members of the LGBTQ community, nor do they claim to be.

But there was also something else: I didn't want to give others the opportunity to explain my sexuality *to me*. Telling people I was confused and questioning did just that. The last thing I needed was another gay man pedantically saying, "You're definitely gay, sweetie," then trying to kiss me. Like, I would prefer if you didn't use my confusion and

---

*Lesbian, gay, bisexual, transgender, queer, questioning, intersex, pansexual, two-spirit, asexual, ally

vulnerability to take sexual advantage of me. I know that's a tough ask, but could you not?

So, straight and in denial I was. I sunk my teeth into that identity and remained there until my therapist illuminated another option. (Spoiler: It starts with a *b*.)

While I undoubtedly had my personal aversion to confusion, we, as a society, need to let people of all ages be confused. Actually—we need to give people the option to explore freely, without judgment or labels. Really, that's all I was doing. I was exploring elements of my sexuality until I figured out that I'm a greedy bisexual stereotype who wants it all. But I needed to get there in my own way, on my own time.

Whereas confusion is passive, exploration is active. Exploration is fun and exciting. Confusion is, well, confusing. While I didn't need cocaine to explore, I did need it to break the anxiety-inducing cycle of confusion.

To be honest, I still get a little sloshed from time to time when I have sex with men. If I can't get hard because of whiskey dick, I plop down on my stomach and prop my ass up in the air. It's still a fun time! Now, however, I have a lot of sober sex with men, too. I have sex sober even when I'm nervous about trying a kink I never have before. I have sober sex when I'm excited to explore something completely novel. Because only when you have sex sober can you start really understanding who you are and what you want. And what I really want, what I've always wanted, is to be able to enjoy the ass that launched one thousand ships.

CHAPTER 5

WHY ARE WE SO BAD AT HANDLING REJECTION?

There are at least 250 people reading this book who are thinking to themselves: *Are you kidding me? How is Zach writing this? He's a self-centered asshole who treats his partners like garbage.* These are people who know me biblically. While this may seem like a lot of folks who hate my guts, I've had sex with about two thousand people, so that is a 12.5 percent hate rate—which, honestly, not bad.

Out of all my past lovers who think I'm a trash person, I'd say I was an actual dick to about thirty of them. I'll own up to that (and I'm sorry, everyone!).

In most other cases, I think almost all feelings of scorn after a relationship boil down to one thing: rejection. Specifically, that most people are not good at handling rejection. I get it. I used to be terrified of sexual and romantic rejection to the point where I couldn't even talk to a person I found attractive. I'd freeze worse than a self-proclaimed vers bottom when he's asked to top.

Few people handle rejection well, which is interesting when you consider the experience's universality. We have all been rejected, excluding, perhaps, Michael B. Jordan. Still, it hurts, and even though we shouldn't, we can't help but take it personally. We extrapolate that if this person doesn't like me, *everyone* dislikes me. Or they dislike the "real" me—the me at my core. Or we think that we must be unattractive. It's our big nose, thin lips, acne, weight, or bald spot. We're too loud, too quiet, too this, too that. Simply put, rejection can feel like an attack on who we are.

For as bad as we are at handling *being* rejected, we're often worse at rejecting folks. Yet again, a universal experience. We've all rejected others, or at least have wanted to reject others—whether we've done so successfully is another issue. My inability to reject people the "right way" (directly but kindly) was how I was a jerk. Still, I was not a malicious jerk—not a fuccboi—but a coward. I often put my hookups in an unnerving limbo, left to wonder if I actually liked them, and why I was taking so long to return a single text.

I was never taught how to reject someone properly. Were any of us? As a teenager, I was never lucky enough to reject people because, spoiler, I wasn't the coolest, best-looking kid in high school. Still, I had a pretty decent high school experience despite being sexually confused and effeminate-leaning. I wasn't a social outcast by any means, but I wasn't exactly swatting away attention either. It took years to evolve into the heavily sought-after sex machine I am today.* Most of the time, I was a freakishly tall, gangly kid with braces and incredibly questionable fashion tastes.

Still, I tried to get laid. That's what you do (or at least you're told you're supposed to do) as a teenage boy. But I had zero game, to the point where I read Neil Strauss' *The Game* twice.

I was mortified to talk to girls. The thought of approaching an attractive girl at a party sober was enough to induce a panic attack. This was why I was blitzed most weekends my senior year. I cannot tell you the number of times I told my mom I was sleeping over somewhere because I had a *Super Smash Bros.* tournament that would likely run late, and I didn't want to drive after the legal California curfew for minors.†

---

*In the words of Beyoncé: "Some call it arrogant; I call it confident."
†That was only true half the time.

But after about seven shots, I had the courage to talk to girls and it rarely went well—few things go well after seven shots. So I got rejected, over and over again. Each rejection didn't make me stronger. I didn't think to myself, *Look! It doesn't matter. You got rejected and nothing has changed in your life.* Instead, they accumulated, and I took each as a measurement of my self-worth. When rejection becomes an unbreakable pattern, it's challenging to shrug it off as only one opinion.

My brother Alex reassured me that this would all change when I got to college. Though I didn't believe him, he was right. At Vassar, I wasn't the kid who had braces for seven years—I had them taken off right before stepping foot on campus—rather, I was the kid with the million-dollar smile. It also helped that Vassar's student body is very queer; quickly, I gained the reputation of one of the few "straight" (lol!) men who fucked. But honestly, the most likely reason women (and guys and nonbinary babes) were DTF? It was college. All of us were getting hammered and trying to fuck because IT WAS COLLEGE. Do you think I went for an education? I went to get my dick wet! College is literally the most expensive sex worker I've ever paid for. Two hundred and fifty thousand dollars to get laid! I usually pay $250!

For the first time in my life, I had women hitting on me aggressively— *really* aggressively—and I had no idea how to respond. I would just fuck them, even if I wasn't attracted to them, even if I found them annoying, even if I knew it would be a one-night stand and they clearly wanted more.

There was one rather unlucky woman I slept with in the first few weeks of arriving at Vassar. She was the third woman I had sex with, and the only woman I'd had sex with who wasn't my girlfriend. She was also my first one-night stand. She didn't go to Vassar; she went to a nearby university in the Hudson Valley. And now that I think about it, I couldn't for the life of me tell you what she was doing on campus alone, besides cruising for dick. (Good for her!)

I met her at a little house party, where she was sitting all alone. She was attractive, but not intimidatingly so. I introduced myself.

"Kiara," she replied. While she had a quiet voice, she wasn't shy—maybe a little socially awkward, but who wasn't at eighteen?

"How's your night going?" I asked.

"Better now," she said with a smile.

"So is mine." I smiled back.

We were flirting. There was banter! We were making eye contact, then she'd look away and blush before looking back at me. Was I killing it? Yes, almost certainly.* A few sentences later, there was a long, awkward pause.

"I just want to get fucked-up and have some fun. There's no alcohol here," she said, breaking the silence.

"Well, we can drink back at mine if you want."

"Yeah, I'd like that," she said.

This was when my heart started pumping. *We're definitely having sex, right? There is no other way to interpret this.*

We had one, maybe two drinks at my place before we were making out. Her top and pants were off and so were mine. When I went to cup her breast under her bra, she swatted my hand away. "Uh-uh," she said.

"Ah, I'm so sorry!" I said.

We kept kissing, she now on top of me. She then said, "I want you inside of me so badly." I was a little confused because she didn't want to go to second base, so a homer seemed out of the question. But I grabbed a condom. Then she said, "No, let's not have sex," so we went back to making out. A few minutes later she told me again that she wanted me inside her. Again I agreed, but then she rescinded. On the third time

---

*I'm aware that saying I was "killing it" after all of seven words is audacious, but by eighteen-year-old Zach standards, I was indeed "killing it."

she asked, I stopped to say, "All right, I am very confused. What do you want to do?"

"I really do want to have sex, but I don't want to be a slut," she said.

"I don't think having sex makes you a slut. If you want to, I feel like you should," I replied.

Cut to us having fantastic fucking sex. Everything was going well until the end . . . the condom broke, or so I thought. In hindsight, I realize she was really wet and actually came. I had never made a woman cum before. (Sorry to my first two girlfriends!) Because I had never made a woman that wet, I assumed that the condom broke. (Clearly, I had a great sex education.) But when I looked for a hole or a tear, I couldn't find one.

Well, this led to an awkward conversation about taking the morning-after pill and her disclosing that her mother didn't want her to go to college. She just wanted her to find a good man, settle down, and raise a family. Well, that freaked me out. She then suggested that if we had a kid, we could name them Skyler. This, again, caused panic. She then proceeded to tell me that she had a boyfriend in New York *City* but I could be her New York *state* boyfriend. I didn't realize she was cheating on her boyfriend either, which didn't make me feel great about myself. Also, her dad thinks she's a virgin and if he ever found out she wasn't, he would find me and beat my ass. Fabulous.

I did not sleep that night. All I could think was: My life is ruined. I was going to get beat up and have to raise a kid named *Skyler*. Back then, I also had a HUGE fear of STIs,* so I went to a clinic. Kiara took the morning-after pill, and I actually set an alarm to text her at 4:00 A.M. to remind her to take the second pill.

After that, she'd hit me up to hang, and I did not reply. (In modern parlance, we call this ghosting.) Not only that, I told anyone who would

---

*Wait till you get to later chapters . . . So much growth!

listen about this "crazy" girl I had slept with. I'm not proud of doing the one thing she was afraid of: labeling her a slut, and a crazy one at that.

Was she a little off? Yes, her behavior was a bit alarming. Did that give me the right to share this story with everyone and brand her with a reputation? Did it give me the right to belittle her? No, absolutely not. In truth, I was only sharing this story to make myself seem cool. I wanted to feel like a big man. I had just had my first one-night stand and wanted the world to know that Zach was fuckable. She must have figured out I was sharing her story because I did see her on campus twice after our hook-up. (Again, unclear what she was doing there since "She doesn't even go here!") And those two times I saw her, she looked me dead in the eyes with a fury and proceeded to bolt out of the room.

I'm no longer sharing this story to brag, nor to illustrate how "fuck-able" I am or how "crazy" she was. (An aside: Guys, seriously, don't call women "crazy." It's fucked-up. But please do call me "fuckable.") I'm sharing this story because it set a precedent for my future one-night stands. I would have sex with someone, and for some reason or another, not want to fuck them again—or even *see* them around—but I didn't know how to gracefully navigate the situation.

I didn't even know how to say no to sleeping with someone. I'd never needed a script for this in the past. I did my fair share of mental gymnastics, too: *Who was I to reject these women?* I'd been rejected; I knew how devastating that felt, how much it stung, how much I'd do anything—even sleeping with people I didn't want to sleep with—to avoid causing that hurt. The logic isn't sound, but it sure felt that way.

So, rather than outright saying I wasn't interested, what I did was far worse. I would have sex with women and then try to avoid them. When they texted me, I knew I shouldn't ghost like I had with Kiara, so instead I would slowly peter out. I'd wait a day or two and then reply curtly, "Sorry, I'm really busy." Sooner or later, they'd get the hint, and we'd spend the rest of college avoiding eye contact whenever we found ourselves in the same room.

I rationalized my crummy behavior well. *How did they not pick up on my clear, uncomfortable body language when they were flirting and instead kept being sexually aggressive? That's on them! What gave them the impression that having mediocre sex while hammered would somehow lead to a romantic relationship?*

While I think the latter question is valid, my repeated decision to avoid and send curt texts remains egregious. Why was it so hard to simply say, "Hey! I had a ton of fun last night, but I think that was just going to be a one-time thing"?

No one had ever suggested that was the right way to approach the situation. If someone had, I'd have thought they were joking. I would have insisted that being so direct makes me sound like *more* of an asshole. They'd end up feeling used and undoubtedly hate me. Nobody wins! At least this way, I save them from dealing with the pain of being outright rejected and the awkwardness that would undoubtedly ensue. Wasn't that better? (It was not.)

While I was incapable of being straight with them (sorry, had to), there was a time when I was forced to be direct. In the dining hall, a woman I had had yet another drunken one-night stand with beelined over to me to ask for a more official date. I said I had a bunch of essays coming up and didn't have time to hang. She suggested a library date, as she had deadlines, too, but I said I liked working alone without distractions. She insisted that she wouldn't bother me; we could just work quietly side by side, so I finally said, "Look, I just don't see this going anywhere."

"Wow," she said, nodding while slowly walking away. "You're a real piece of work."

I was left paralyzed, feeling like a terrible person. But then that pitiful self-loathing turned into anger. *Why did she come up to me in the dining hall? Why didn't she take my hints? And why did she expect something more when we drunkenly made out in a basement after only saying a handful of words and had average sex? Besides, she left right after. She didn't even spend the night!*

In hindsight, I know my anger was an internalized response to feeling like a jerk. Instead of reflecting on how I could have handled the situation better, it was simpler to blame her for not picking up cues. Still, there is something to be said about taking the hint. I couldn't tell you the number of times a friend has told me a story about someone they're seeing who's clearly not interested in them; I tell them to read the signs and move along—but they don't. It's hard, though. Taking the hint means facing rejection.

This is a point worth belaboring: Rejection is hella painful, and there's actually a biological reason behind it. Rejection fires up the same parts in your brain as physical pain. Over the past two decades, count-less studies have illustrated a neural overlap between social rejection and physical pain. One of the first, a 2006 study published in the journal *Pain*—which has to be the best name of any academic journal—showed participants playing a virtual game of "pass the ball" on a computer. They were put into one of three conditions: inclusion, non-inclusion, and overt exclusion.

As described in the study: "Individuals in the inclusion condition played the interactive ball-tossing game for the entire time. Participants in the non-inclusion condition were told that, due to some technical difficulties in connecting to the two other players, they could watch the other two players play, but would not actually be able to play with them. Individuals in the overt exclusion condition were included in the game for the first fifty seconds of the game and then excluded for the duration of the game, when the two virtual players stopped throwing them the ball."

Now, I'm grossly oversimplifying this study, but in the discussion section the researchers note, "These findings support the idea that pain distress and social distress rely on some of the same computational substrates by demonstrating that sensitivity to one type of distressing experience is directly related to sensitivity to the other." This helps explain why rejection is so painful (both physically and emotionally) and why we handle it so poorly.

X X X

My therapist once told me that anger comes from unmet expectations; there's an incongruence between what you want and what you get. I thought that was such a simple definition of anger.

In the case of cafeteria girl, she wanted me but I didn't want her. So she got angry, either from the rejection itself, how I delivered the news, or both. And since then, she hasn't been the only one. Multiple sexual partners have accused me of using them for sex, being careless with their feelings, and leading them on.

This is why people ghost! People don't want to deal with the thorny process of rejecting someone. They don't want to be chewed out and called an asshole or witness an intense emotional response. They also don't want to get dragged into a longer conversation, which has happened to me quite a few times. Unpopular opinion: If you're in the early stages of dating, say one to four dates, I don't think a larger conversation is warranted. Yes, you deserve a kind and direct text or phone call, but nothing beyond that. After all, you weren't looking at wedding registries! You might not even know their middle (or last) name. All you know is that they're a Libra and that you have a "thing" for air signs.

Maybe if we had healthier ways to internalize and respond to rejection, there'd be less of an incentive to cut ties without warning.

Instead, because no one wants to receive the wrath of someone we had two slightly above average dates with, we never text back. On the other hand, when *we* are rejected kindly, our response is still often anger. I'm sorry, but you can't have it both ways—and this is me, a bisexual, saying this!

I hope I don't sound like I'm victim-blaming. Yes, you are entitled to your feelings, including anger. But I do hope we can learn to put things into perspective if we're getting rejected after a one-night stand or couple of dates. I want us to get in the habit of responding to a kind rejection text with, "What a bummer, but I appreciate you being honest and direct with me."

That said, we also need to get better at letting people feel their emotions, even when those (negative) emotions are directed toward us. These days, I'm better at handling rejection, but I still struggle with rejecting others out of fear of their response. There are times when I should say, "Hey, I had a fun time connecting, but I don't think we're a match." Yet, I don't always. (I am working on this in therapy!)

I continuously wrestle with "doing the right thing" because, no matter how hard I try, I still feel like a piece of shit when someone lashes out. Often, they'll say I have zero right being a sex and relationship advice columnist. I'm not ethical the way I claim to be, and I'm trash like every other fuccboi. When this happens, I don't feel "good" about my decision to be direct. Quite the opposite: I'm encouraged to *not* be direct the next time I'm in a similar scenario.

Still, I try to tell myself that if I am entitled not to want to date or sleep with someone again, they're entitled to think I'm an asshole. That's something I have to live with. While I know I'm not responsible for their feelings, it still sucks knowing that I hurt a good person whose only crime was liking someone who didn't like them back, or at least not how they wanted to be liked.

I also try to remember that while I see my partner's initial reaction, I don't know how they're feeling two days, two weeks, or two months after. Odds are, they're happy I didn't draw out our mismatched relationship longer. Maybe they found a perfect partner right after me. Even if they don't come around two months later and still pray I choke on a croissant, that's okay; that's their choice.

I wish I could give you some actionable advice about how to give and respond to rejection more productively. But beyond encouraging you not to take it personally, and, in the moment, taking a few deep breaths, so you can "respond" rather than "react"—I'm not sure what else there is. (Think of "reacting" as being an instinctive, knee-jerk response caused by overwhelming emotions. Whereas "responding" is a more thoughtful approach, considering the desired outcome. Reacting is emotional, whereas responding is emotional intelligence.)

Nevertheless, don't let fear or rejection stop you from having sex and finding love. Don't let the pain, uncomfortable conversations, or getting chewed out turn you into a jaded old queen. Allow yourself to feel your emotions, give space for others to feel theirs, and then move right along. As Lady Gaga once said, there can be one hundred people in a room, and ninety-nine reject you, but all it takes is one.* And that person can change your whole life.

---

*Unless you're poly, at which point you need maybe two to four people.

CHAPTER 6

THERAPY IS(N'T) HELPING

I n my long, illustrious mental health career, I've had a total of five therapists and two psychiatrists. My second therapist, the one I had right after college, was top-notch. He worked to undue the harm caused by my pre-college psychiatrist, Dr. Schmuck.

Dr. Schmuck exemplified mediocrity. He did the bare minimum: run through the same set of twelve diagnostic questions and prescribe medication. I was there for no more than seventeen minutes, and each session cost two hundred dollars out of pocket. (The American medical system clearly values and prioritizes mental health.)

There were only two things I liked about seeing him. One, he gave me life-saving drugs that significantly improved my OCD. Two, he had whimsical furniture that the fictional love child of Disney and Gaudí designed.

When I was about fifteen, I decided to switch up the flow of our session. Sitting in the bright yellow, 1970s-style swivel hand chair, I broke his usual line of questioning to inquire if I may ask him a question.

Dr. Shmuck looked up from his notepad, adjusted his tortoiseshell glasses, and said, "Proceed."

"I—I." I couldn't get the words out. He sat quietly as I struggled to finally ask, "How do I know if I'm gay?"

Without missing a beat, he replied, "Well, do you like women?"

"Yes!" I said. It was the truth. I did like women.

"Then you're not gay," he said matter-of-factly.

"Could I be bisexual?" I knew about bisexuality from the LGBTQ acronym, but my only real encounter with bisexuality was with a girl a year older than me. She asked me out on a date, and we had dinner at the Cheesecake Factory at the Sherman Oaks Galleria. At one point in the evening, while I was eating more than a human stomach could possibly consume, she told me that she was bisexual. I freaked out and assumed that she must be a sexual deviant. After the date, whenever I saw her at school, I would run the other way.*

"No, bisexuality doesn't exist in men," Dr. S replied.

For years, rage consumed me whenever I replayed this conversation. *Imagine if he said bisexuality is valid? Imagine if instead of dismissing me, he explored it further with literally any follow-up question.* Hearing that bisexuality wasn't real from the medical professional who'd been treating me for the past seven years undoubtedly contributed to my confusion, anxiety, and alcohol abuse in college. He set me back nearly a decade!

Now, however, I can understand where he was coming from. This whole debacle took place in 2006, just a few months after the controversial Northwestern study titled "Sexual Arousal Patterns of Bisexual Men" concluded, "With respect to sexual arousal and attraction, it remains to be shown that male bisexuality exists." This study was covered by multiple outlets, including the *New York Times*, in a piece titled "Straight, Gay or Lying? Bisexuality Revisited."

In 2011, the same researchers conducted another study, aptly titled "Sexual Arousal Patterns of Bisexual Men Revisited," which concluded that bi men do, in fact, exist. The *Times* also covered the second study in a piece titled "No Surprise for Bisexual Men: Report Indicates They Exist."†

This partially explains why my psychiatrist quickly dismissed

---

*Perhaps, just perhaps, I was running from myself . . .

†It's like, thanks guys, but also go fuck yourselves. I'm going to get an NIH-funded grant to conduct my study: "Do Researchers at Northwestern Actually Exist?"

me. However, I would suspect that the main reason had to do with my OCD. He likely thought I was experiencing sexual orientation OCD (SO-OCD), a subtype of OCD characterized by intrusive thoughts and compulsive behaviors around your own sexual orientation. People with SO-OCD question their sexuality to the point where it can ruin their and their family's lives. And more often than not, people who experience SO-OCD are straight. They're obsessing for no reason!

So treating gay/bi patients with OCD poses unique problems. Generally, you don't want to validate SO-OCD obsessions, but in my case, I *was* actually queer,* so some validation and further exploration—anything at all—would have been helpful.

Alas, my perfectly mediocre psychiatrist did what he always did—treated me as a member of a group and not as an individual. While I was processing his dismissal of my possible bisexuality, he took my silence as an opportunity to return to his clipboard and continue his laundry list of usual questions.

Luckily, when I was twenty-two, I could pick my own therapist. I worked at Massachusetts General Hospital as a smoking cessation researcher and had fabulous health insurance, so my options were seemingly limitless. Despite identifying as straight, I went on the *Psychology Today* website and filtered my therapist search by "LGBTQ." Clearly, the queer part of me was backseat driving.

I found this preppy-looking fifty-year-old gay man who previously worked as an attorney. On our preliminary call, I told him that I liked that he used to be a lawyer because I wanted him to be blunt with me. I explained how I hate hearing "What do you think?" because, by the time I've brought up an issue with a therapist, I've thought about it obsessively and need a new perspective. I also made clear that when I

---

*Please refer back to the picture with my limp wrist and umbrella behind my ear.

ask for advice directly, I want advice. I don't care if it leads to chaos. I will not get mad at him if he accidentally gives me advice that leads to an apocalypse—or worse, Billy Porter coming out as straight—I *need* to hear what someone else has to say.

I'm aware this goes against how therapists are trained. They're not advice givers. They don't tell clients what to do. They help each client decide what's best for them by asking a range of questions and probing certain comments more than others. Nevertheless, he promised to be more forthcoming with me than with other clients.

In my first session, I launched into an endless monologue on being confused about my sexuality. He couldn't get a word in edgewise. I started from my first same-sex experience, when I was seven years old, to my most recent same-sex experience, seven days prior. In the second session, I was repeating a variation of the same monologue when he interrupted me.

"Zach, you said you wanted me to be blunt with you, so I would like to be blunt."

"Please," I said.

"When we use the word 'confused' in the context of a person's sexuality, it means something very specific, and it's not what you're describing." I nodded, waiting for him to continue. "You seem very clearly bisexual. Is there something I'm missing?"

"That doesn't actually exist in men," I quickly snapped back.

"Zach, you're too smart to think that," he replied. Honestly, I don't think he could have provided a better response.

Hearing this from a third party—a therapist no less—made bisexuality a real, concrete option. There was this word, this identity, that perfectly encapsulated what I'd been thinking and feeling since I was a kid. Ironically, it was a word that I was familiar with—a word that I had referenced countless times whenever I said LGBTQ. But because I hadn't met another out bisexual man, and every time I heard male bisexuality discussed it was mocked and dismissed, it hadn't seemed like a real possibility.

But now a therapist wasn't just saying bisexuality was a viable possibility; he was proclaiming that I was *obviously* bisexual. After countless sleepless nights, I could finally take the bisexual option.*

XXX

Everything about therapy is a pain in the ass. Finding a therapist who accepts your insurance is harder than finding a top at a Charli XCX concert. The growing number of websites and apps that claim to easily connect you with a mental health counselor are often useless because they don't attack the issue at the source: Therapy is a business. Therapists need to get paid, and since the government doesn't value mental health, you, the person seeking therapy, will have to pay.

If you don't have insurance, you need to find a therapist who works on a sliding scale. Some do, but rarely does it cost the same as a co-pay. And let's say you do find a therapist who doesn't charge an arm and a leg. They typically have one slot available between three thirty and four fifteen Wednesday mornings every other week.

And I'm just talking about finding *any* therapist. If you're queer, you'll likely want a queer-affirming therapist. If you're poly, you'll want a therapist specializing in alternative lifestyles. If you're a woman who's experienced sexual trauma, you may want a female therapist, and so on.

Then, of course, even when you find a therapist, they're not always great (hello, Dr. Schmuck!). Mental health professionals can cause serious harm. You're in such a vulnerable headspace in therapy, and you

---

*I'm borrowing the "option" language from Fritz Klein, the most prominent bisexual researcher in the world. His book, *The Bisexual Option,* is worth reading for the historical perspective alone. He also developed the Klein Sexual Orientation Grid, which is far more thorough than the Kinsey Scale.

trust your therapist. So when they say something that's wildly incorrect, we are quick to take it as the word of God. But let us not forget that therapists are not gods; they are people who make mistakes, have bad days, and say things they shouldn't. They can be staunchly sex-negative. They can victim-blame survivors of assault. They can kink-shame, slut-shame, and simply shame-shame.

Or they're just bad. I once dropped a therapist after our second session because his advice for my anxiety was to take ten big inhales and ten big exhales. I was not paying $150 a session for him to tell me to breathe. Besides, I am *great* at breathing; how else do you think I manage to take ten-inch dicks?

Since therapy can be helpful, detrimental, or a waste of time and money, it's crucial to find the *right* therapist and to remember that you are capable of independent critical thought. If they say something about how you process your emotions or communicate with partners, that doesn't automatically make it true.

Okay, now let's say you do find a fantastic therapist who's an excellent fit for your needs. You then need to put in the work. You need to dig deep, face your fears, and open up. That's no easy feat, especially for men, and double especially for men conditioned to stoicism. Some men have become so accustomed to suppressing their feelings they struggle to recognize, label, emote, and express themselves. This is called "normative male alexithymia." That's why it's not always as simple as "my boyfriend won't open up to me." He's literally lost the ability to do so.

This all speaks to why it's so important to find the right therapist. Anyone looking to understand their feelings and improve their communication skills needs one. (Spoiler: This is everyone on the planet.)

Now, I would be a real douche nozzle if I noted all the ways therapy is cost- or otherwise prohibitive and then said, but get your ass into it! I understand many people simply can't find or afford a therapist.

Luckily, you bought the book of a sex and relationship columnist who's been in therapy for over two decades. I've gone ahead and distilled my twentysomething years of therapy into seven tips. (We all still secretly love a listicle, or at least I hope so.)

1. Figure out what you want, and ask for it kindly.

Many of us have been taught that it's selfish to ask for what we want. (This is truer for women than men.) However, there is nothing wrong with asking for what you want, whether it's more commitment from a partner, a raise at work, or your mother to stop calling you every day. I know it can be hard to find your voice and assert yourself. And while many of us have no problems standing up for friends or loved ones, we struggle when it comes to advocating for ourselves.

I used to be much more of a people pleaser than I am now, which many of my newer friends may find hard to believe. I mean, I still please people sexually, but I'm less likely to acquiesce to ridiculous demands or outlandish behavior, and I'm much more likely to ask for what I want. I never had an epiphany or some pivotal experience that gave me the courage to change my behavior. Rather, I reached a point where I was okay with losing people. I realized that if I ask for something, whether it's to be treated a certain way or for a raise or for more commitment in a relationship, and I didn't get the answer I had hoped for, I would be okay. My world would not shatter.

It helps if you ask kindly for what you want. If you're a dick when you ask for what you want, well then, you're a dick. You can always express your wants and desires compassionately with the other person in mind. And as basic as this may sound, it's by using good old-fashioned "I" statements.

For example, "I sometimes feel as if I am taken for granted. Little things like saying 'thank you' more, or taking out the trash without me asking, would help make *me* feel more appreciated." The translation of this is: "You're an ungrateful asshole who doesn't notice everything I do for you; you can't even be bothered to say 'thanks,' the simplest common courtesy. Seriously, what is wrong with you?"

But you see how the "I feel" approach works a lot better? It's also, dare I say, a trap that works in your favor because you can't argue with someone's feelings. It's how they feel.

It also helps to accept rejection gracefully. (Oh, you thought I was done talking about rejection?) Don't freak out when you get a no to something you wanted. Just as you are allowed to ask for things, they're allowed to decline. Don't try to negotiate. Simply accept their no the first time around. If it's something that you really need, well, you now have that information and can proceed accordingly. If someone you're dating says that they have no desire to be monogamous with you, then you decide whether you want to continue the relationship with them. (If you're very monogamous-oriented, I'd suggest not, but you're allowed to make your own mistakes.) If your boss doesn't give you that raise, then look for other jobs where you feel more fairly compensated. When you look at no or rejection as information rather than an attack on your self-worth, you're able to process it clearly and use this information to go and get what you want. That's the end goal. That said, when you start asking kindly for what you want, you might be surprised by how often you get it.

2. Figure out when you should address issues.

Some people are quick to anger and will pop off at the drop of a hat. Even if they were wronged, and their feelings are valid, they'll poorly express themselves through yelling and blame. If this sounds like you, I suggest sleeping on it, collecting your thoughts, and addressing the issue later, when you're able to more calmly and constructively express yourself.

Or you might be like me and feel very uncomfortable with your anger. Instead of lashing out at others, I turn inward and shut down. I stew on the issue for a few days, and by the time I end up talking about it with my partner, I've turned it into this huge ordeal, when actually, it was likely a simple miscommunication.

Recently, a partner and I were playing an offensive "Would you rather?" card game. The prompt was picking between being a heroin addict or having HIV. My partner said she'd rather be a heroin addict, and I lost it. I have spent so much of my work attempting to destigmatize people living with HIV, preaching how HIV isn't a death sentence anymore, and educating folks about undetectable viral loads.* Yet, there she was saying she'd rather be a heroin addict than have a virus that's easier to manage than diabetes. I spent the rest of the night sulking, and when we did finally have a talk about it, my rage had morphed into resentment. I blew up at her, and she was like, "Zach, I'm sorry. It was a game. I wasn't thinking, and I'm not as knowledgeable as you about HIV. Send me some articles you've written so that I can learn."

Clearly communicating about that more levelheadedly would have been better than my stewing in anger for days. I am trying to get better at addressing things as they happen. It's challenging because it can take me a moment to process what's going on, but I've started to say, "What did you mean by that?" or, "I feel like you ignored what I said."

This is new for me because it goes against my natural tendencies to remove myself from heated conflict. But in that situation, mild to moderate conflict in the moment was better than my freaking out for a week, during which I felt disconnected from and disdain for my partner.

---

*Often referred to as undetectable equals untransmittable, or U=U, those living with HIV who have an undetectable viral load—meaning levels of HIV in the blood are below the threshold for detection—cannot transmit the virus.

3. People don't respond well to conflict in real time.

Similarly, it's necessary to acknowledge that most people don't respond well to conflict as it unfolds. If they feel attacked, what they say in the heat of the moment could be less than kind. They also may respond by attacking back. (This again is why "I" statements are so valuable.) Or they respond by crying. Neither are productive responses—the person who's bringing up the issue shouldn't also play the consoler. You're bringing up something that hurt you; *you* should be the one getting consoled.

So it's crucial to have some time away after a conflict to recollect and think things over. It's often the second or third time you discuss an issue when things start getting resolved. Expect and even encourage having conversations about an issue multiple times.

4. You're not (usually) responsible for people's feelings.

I add "usually" because these aphorisms are sometimes taken out of context. I've known people to be cruel and use non-responsibility as a pithy justification for their behavior. It's like, no, your demonstration of radical self-care actually *was* selfish and mean. Your unnecessarily brutal comments *can* make someone feel worthless, and you *are* responsible for their feelings.

However, when you are honest *and* kind, you're not responsible. Similarly, when you're up-front with your intentions—this is particularly true when it comes to dating and sex—you don't need to feel accountable for someone else's reaction.

We are quick to blame ourselves or others when something goes awry in a relationship, but there's often no one to blame. You simply had incompatible desires and needs. Blame comes from a place of hurt and frustration; logic isn't often a part of the equation. That's okay. People are allowed to feel any way they please—that's not on you to justify or solve.

5. This, too, shall pass.

I have spent countless sleepless nights worrying about something I thought would ruin my life. I couldn't tell you what 99 percent of these worries concerned. As for the 1 percent of troubling things I do remember? Well, I'm still here. My life hasn't ended. I'm not saying I haven't dealt with some serious shit. I have—we all have—but I'm alive. I'm here. I'm happy. Most worries, eventually, do pass. I'm not going to say you're stronger for it. I would much rather have not dealt with troubling hardships. But I will say you will be better equipped to handle similar challenges when they arise in the future.

It's why every subsequent relationship gets a *little* bit better. Or, at least, we hopefully don't make the same mistakes in each new relationship. We worry a little bit less. We're more certain of their love for us. We know that if someone we love leaves us, however painful it may be, the pain shall pass. We'll still be here and back on Scruff in no time.

6. Extend your empathy beyond things you understand.

When I get into a fight or argument with someone, I can easily forgive them if I know I would have (mis)behaved the same way in their situation. But when someone behaves in a manner that's foreign to me, I struggle to put myself in their shoes. I find it challenging to understand where they're coming from, so I subsequently struggle to forgive.

Recently, I've tried to extend my empathy to a type of person I don't and will never understand: late people. I used to loathe people who run late. I found it both infuriating and disrespectful. My interpretation was that they don't value my time, and I thought it made them immature. Like, how have you made it to thirty and don't allot extra time because the subway system cannot be trusted? How are you always late? It's not cute. It's not a quirky trait. It's just rude.

But that is just the way some people are wired.* They are seemingly incapable of being on time, and it's not because they don't value my time. They are just, well, late. I don't get it. I really, *really* don't get it, but I'm doing my best to extend empathy to those pieces of shit who consistently run late. (Clearly, I'm still working on it.) And this same logic can be applied in relationships. You don't always have to understand everything to accept and forgive.

7. Shame is a harmful emotion.

A quick reminder of the difference between guilt and shame. Put simply, guilt is "I did a bad thing," whereas shame is "I am a bad person."

Guilt has benefits. If you do something horrible to a partner, you should feel guilty. The nauseating feelings accompanying guilt deter you from repeating mistakes. It's a form of negative reinforcement (which you may remember from your intro to psychology course is different from punishment). This is all hunky-dory as long as your guilt isn't crippling, and you can move past it.

Feeling shame—believing that *you* are wrong—is detrimental. It doesn't encourage positive behavior. Rather, it facilitates self-loathing. And self-loathing causes a slew of negative consequences and harmful behavior: drug abuse, alcoholism, depression, anxiety, rage—all that good stuff!

---

*Running late is actually a common indicator of neurodiversity, specifically ADD/ADHD.

Shame is a tool that people in power use to exert control. Religious conservatives use shame to prevent queer people from living joyfully and authentically. Men slut-shame women to keep women tethered to men. We feel shame for not working overtime because capitalism has told us that our worth is derived from our output. Honestly, shame is a pretty genius method to control the masses.

So never feel shame. Never think that your mere existence is somehow wrong. Instead, when you feel shame, think about *why* you're feeling it. Think about who or what is trying to control you. When you better understand the root cause of your shame, you'll be able to realize it has nothing to do with you and all to do with some ridiculous societal pressures—which hinder, not help. From there, it's much easier to tell your shame to go fuck itself.

X X X

I don't mean to give the impression that I have everything figured out. I don't. But I have come a long way, and there is one thing in particular I do better than the vast majority of the population: Live shamelessly. I'm shameless when I have sex. I'm shameless when I ask for raises. I'm shameless when I ask for what I want.*

This shamelessness didn't happen overnight, but I do know coming out and embracing my bisexuality definitely pushed me forward. I had spent years uncertain of what I wanted while managing to deny myself of it. After I came out, I wanted to *live*. I wanted it all. I wanted multiple partners, so I explored polyamory. I wanted to write about sex, so I quit my job at Massachusetts General Hospital, decided against pursuing a PhD in clinical psychology, and instead wrote stupid, gay listicles that

---

*As my favorite tote reads: "Carry yourself with the confidence of a mediocre white man."

were more gifs than words. But you know what? That's what I wanted. That brought me joy and to where I am today.

Many people still think that being shameless is a bad thing. They think it means you have no moral compass, or you lack care for others. That's not what it means at all. All it means is being absent of shame because shame doesn't bring anything positive to your life. Only once you've become shameless can you start being truly fulfilled and happy. At the end of the day, that's all I want for myself. All I want for you. And as corny as it may sound, all I want for the world.

Now I know this advice is not as thorough as therapy, but for the price of this book, I'd say it's not too shabby.

CHAPTER 7

MY LIGHTBULB MOMENT

By the age of twenty-three, I had read too much queer theory for my own good. I had made a distinction between my sexual and romantic attractions, convincing myself I was bi-sexual (notice the hyphen)* but hetero-romantic, meaning that I was sexually attracted to men, women, and non-binary folks but could only date and love women. Yes, I had fucked the ass that launched a thousand ships, but my boat for the sea of male romance was still docked in the harbor.

That is until I met George one weekend in Provincetown in the autumn of 2014.

Back then, I wasn't the confident, shameless Boyslut you've come to know and ~~love~~ tolerate. How could I have been? I was in denial and actively repressing a huge part of myself. This was why I forged a love-hate relationship with Provincetown that kept me coming back for more. Provincetown, or P-Town if you're queer, is a gay mecca located at the tip of Cape Cod. The gays are OUT and about in their cutoff jean shorts, crop tops, and sequin heels. They're kissing openly in the streets and getting railed at the Dick Dock, unabashedly embracing their sexuality and identity.

It was strange being confused and partially closeted in a town where the majority of people are confident and openly gay. Even though at times I felt uncomfortable being a "straight" man in P-Town, I think I subconsciously knew it was good for me to be there—to see how

---

*"Bisexual" without the hyphen indicates both a romantic and sexual attraction to multiple genders, whereas "bi-sexual" indicates solely sexual attraction and "bi-romantic" indicates solely romantic attraction.

joyous my life could be if I embraced my sexuality. So I kept returning. (It didn't hurt that I had gay uncles who lived there, so I had a place to crash for free.)

I almost didn't go out the night I met George. I had just finished watching an unremarkable film in town with my uncles. When I told them I wanted to head back to their place, one insisted that I should go out. When I said that he and his husband should hit the bars with me, he laughed. "We're old farts."

I wasn't used to going out alone, and this was during my liquid-courage era, when I needed to be hammered to talk to potential hook-ups. To go to a gay bar alone when you're straight, but also not, but kinda are, sets off a whole slew of anxieties. But why was I in P-Town? To visit my lovely, supportive guncles? Fuck them! (Just kidding, I love you, Andy and Paul!) I was there to be free and party—at least that's what I told myself. Hell, Andy and Paul told me, too.

So I walked on over to the dance club Atlantic House, or A-House.* A-House has been a staple in P-Town for over forty years, and I'm pretty sure they haven't updated the music once in the past four decades. There's nothing particularly exceptional about the space itself, except for maybe the bathroom, which is covered in cutouts of naked hunks with massive cocks—a classy touch. But no one goes there for the physical space. They go there for the men who aren't plastered to the bathroom walls.

Once inside A-House, I beelined it to the bar. I ordered a double Jack and Diet, pounded it, and proceeded to order two more. In college, I had made a habit of asking myself what the goal of each evening was. Knowing what I want out of a situation helps guide the night. I also noticed it helps me frame how I feel about the evening the next

---

*I'm realizing queers really like to abbreviate things that don't need to be abbreviated.

day. This evening's goal was pretty clear: Try to fuck the impossibly attractive gay men scattered throughout the bar. After all, I was still bi DASH sexual.

It wasn't until my third double Jack and Diet that I noticed George. He had a square, Superman-esque jaw, light blue eyes, massive DSLs, and freckles covering his cheeks. His green button-down shirt was untucked, and the top three buttons were undone, revealing his modest chest hair. Black tattoos with sharp lines covered the rest of his visible body, and he wore a backward baseball cap with a little tuft of strawberry red hair popping out the front. The man loved an accessory, adorned with rings, bracelets, a necklace, and dangly earrings. Last, but certainly not least, his tight jeans were cuffed at the bottom, though that's not where anyone was looking. His ass filled out those jeans, and he knew it.

He was alone at the other side of the bar, laughing as he chatted with the bartender. His sweet laughter carried over the blaring music. After staring him down with zero chill, I saw him move to the dance floor. I had drunk enough liquid courage to follow.

"I love your dangly earrings," I finally said.

"Thanks!" he said emphatically. "Want to step outside to talk? I can't hear you well."

I nodded, thinking to myself that this was going too smoothly. He lit up a cigarette and offered me one. I politely declined.

"Good, you shouldn't smoke. It's bad for you," he said.

We started talking about what brought us to P-Town but quickly transitioned into a deeper, more intimate conversation. While fast, it felt natural. His honesty wasn't abrasive—it was the opposite, a warm welcome. He shared that he grew up in an abusive household until he was fifteen, when he decided to live on his own. He was the first in his family to go to college, where he honed his activism skills to fight for marginalized communities. A year earlier, he got back from the Middle

East, where he was working to help impoverished children with cancer, related to the start-up he headed. (Like, COME on.) He came home to find his husband of four years gone. He had just picked up and left. It led him down a path of overusing alcohol, drugs, and sex, along with an inability to trust.

He spoke so openly and warmly that it was like I had stepped into his life, had walked through it alongside him. The man was a natural-born storyteller. He knew when to let a somber moment sit, and when to pick up with a moment of levity. His effortless charisma was alluring. He had that magic ability to make you feel like you two are the only people in a crowded bar, when in fact some dude was surreptitiously getting his penis sucked mere feet away.

When he asked if I wanted to leave with him, I was like putty in the palm of his calloused man-hands. Strolling down Commercial Street, he whipped out a slingshot and started shooting little rocks at signs. It was such a boyish thing to do, and it only made me like him more. He had layers, and everyone loves an onion.

Back at his place, we went to his bedroom and lay down together.

"Hi," he said. I met his gaze without saying a word. He quickly broke eye contact and flushed. "Sorry, you're just really cute, and I get awkward."

If anyone else had said that to me, I would have known he was playing me—but I trusted him. I believed him. And I was feeling the same way, too. Yes, I felt comfortable in his presence, but I also didn't want to fuck things up. This guy seemed too good to be true.

"Don't be," I said, and our eyes locked again. We both leaned in to kiss—a slow, soft kiss. His lips were slightly chapped, but I didn't mind. It humanized him. I inhaled deeply as I closed my eyes. He wasn't wearing deodorant and his musk was intoxicating.

We undressed. He was wearing boxer briefs—Hanes—nothing flashy, but they fit in all the right places. Looking in his baby blues, I knew this hookup wasn't going to be like my past experiences with men. Those were all about *fucking*, but this felt like the precipice of something more. I just wanted to look at him, touch him, and kiss him—and that's what we did. I mean, I blew him, too, but like, in a romantic way.

He fell asleep in my arms, and the next morning when we awoke, we immediately started kissing, cuddling, and feeling each other. When our stomachs grumbled in unison, we decided to grab some food.

After a shower, we got brunch at a place where he knew the owner and server by name. He invited both of them over later to help him make applesauce with all the fallen apples in his yard. I was pretty sure he'd never hung out with them before, but he seemed happy to invite them over. He was open like that—to new people. To experiencing new friendships.

At brunch, his ability to turn a mundane conversation into a heart-to-heart continued. An innocuous comment about pancake toppings led to his diagnosing me as a yes-man.

"That's good," he said. "I couldn't ever be with anyone who didn't say yes to new adventures—to love."

As I write this now, it's all painfully corny but you have to understand that Provincetown is painfully corny in the best way possible. It's a surreal fantasyland where time stops. Everyone is queer. Everyone is friendly. The bitchy Boston boys who act like they don't know you even though you've met them seven times at Club Café suddenly become your best friends. Your guard is down. It's a prerequisite before stepping off the ferry and onto MacMillan Pier.

I had never been so vulnerable with a man before P-Town. That's the magic of that place. It's why I let myself go, and I didn't hold back. It didn't hurt that we were surrounded by gay couples. Seeing such a public embrace of love, of who people are, encouraged me to do the same.

Was it love? No. But it was more than lust. It was electric; it was potential. After brunch, he walked me back to my uncles' house. I had the ferry scheduled back to the mainland in a few hours.

"I don't know what it is," he said on the steps of my uncles' place. "I can't tell if it's that you're leaving, and I won't ever see you again—or see you again like this—or if it's really something more. But I can see myself with you."

"I know. I feel the same way," I said. I looked into his baby-blue eyes one final time before giving him a long kiss. I turned away as the tears started to well and walked through the front door.

X X X

We never saw each other again. We texted for a few days, but it quickly petered out. He wasn't the most responsive texter, and when I was back in Boston, no longer under P-Town's spell, I felt that I should let it be. Let me not pursue a long-distance relationship with someone I had spent only twenty-four hours with. Let me enjoy it for what it was.

Still, I thought about him often. When I ran into some P-Town friends at a bar a few weeks later, I asked if they knew him. They did. Apparently he was a manipulative abuser who brutally beat his last boyfriend. My friends, too, had nearly identical vulnerable experiences with him where they immediately fell head over heels. Apparently, making people fall in love was his thing.

I was left dumbstruck. First, denial hit. "But he shared about how his husband—"

"Up and left him when he was back from some fake charity nonsense?" my friend interrupted. "Yeah, it took his husband a lot of courage to finally leave that relationship."

"He said that he could—"

"Actually see himself with you? He said the same thing to us."

It turned out he *was* too perfect. His charm wasn't effortless; it was calculated. His vulnerability wasn't genuine. It was a tool to lure guys like me in, and I fell for it—like a fool. But this is where all my years of being closeted actually helped me. I was a master of compartmentalization and holding two cognitively dissonant beliefs together. I don't want to say I was able to "forget" that he was a manipulative abuser—but I could focus on my feelings, which were real. I could despise this man and never talk to him again while also acknowledging he unintentionally did me a huge service. Our meeting taught me to not shy away from my emotions. I could embrace them, even with men. Just with the *right* men.

I had always prided myself on being logical, on understanding that my feelings aren't facts. I needed to approach life this way because if I gave into every feeling I had, my OCD would have continued to consume my life. I would be a bawling mess who perpetually felt guilty. Since I was so used to my feelings leading me astray, it was imperative to control my emotions, whether anger, sadness, or even love.

But controlling my emotions made coming out and accepting myself so tumultuous. Even though we don't conceptualize it as such, our sexuality is simply a bundle of complex feelings. It's the feelings of love you have toward someone. It's the feeling of desire. It's attraction, one of the most complicated feelings. It's lust and joy, but also fear of rejection, unrequited love, and feeling overwhelmed.

Years of therapy and practice led me to avoid feeling overwhelmed, but that same overwhelming sensation I felt with George was also what unlocked something in me: my capability to love a man.

Despite George being an abuser, my initial feelings for him simply could not be suppressed. They couldn't be denied, rationalized, or analyzed with logic. This was a *good* type of overwhelming that could lead to embrace.

I could love a man. My future could include a person of any gender by my side. I just needed to be smart, to balance my emotions and logic. I didn't have to hand out my heart to the first pretty boy with piercing blue eyes who whispered sweet nothings, but I could give it to a man. Better he be one who's genuine, loving, and supportive. I wouldn't wear my heart on my sleeve, but I'd wear it *right* underneath it.

PART III

SEXUAL
SECURITY

CHAPTER 8

"SO . . . YOU'RE ACTUALLY BISEXUAL?"

I thought the hardest part of my sexuality journey was over once I came out as bi. Life would surely become a piece of cake. Gay and straight communities would accept me with open arms, and anyone attracted to men would be open to dating me. Surely, they wouldn't have a single negative or untrue preconceived notion about my sexuality!

I was painfully naive. People have a lot of thoughts when it comes to bisexuality (and pansexuality). My not-so-hot take is that they feel *way* too comfortable expressing them.

To be clear, I'm not sharing how people have responded to my bisexuality in an attempt to evoke pity. This isn't to propagate a "woe is me" mentality—*look how hard it is being a sexy bisexual!* (I'm also aware that I'm a white, muscular, cisgender man, so I come in hot with a number of privileges.) However, bisexuals do have the worst mental and physical health outcomes on nearly every single metric, and I don't think they're addressed nearly enough!*

We experience "double discrimination," which simply means we're often discriminated against by both gay and straight communities. This leads us to feeling alone and like we don't belong.

Well, you are *not* alone, and you *do* belong no matter what (some) monosexuals think. While you can't control what people say or think about

---

*Bisexuals report higher levels of anxiety and depression than their gay and lesbian peers, whose levels are higher than those of heterosexuals, and are at a higher risk for suicide. Bi folks also have poorer overall physical health, more pain, and poorer general health. Bisexual men also have higher rates of eating disorders than both gay and straight men.

you, you luckily can control how you respond. Over my many years of being a "bisexual mega-influencer,"* I've learned the best way to respond to any ignorant (and well-intentioned) nonsense hurled in my direction.

With that said, let me take you on an exhausting journey through the world's reaction to learning that you're bisexual. Enjoy being bewildered, frustrated, and a little bi-furious.

How do you know you're bisexual?

There are two distinct ways someone can ask this question. The first comes from someone questioning their own sexuality. They're asking because they think they might be bisexual.

How I've responded: Personally, it was a journey. Some people know very early on that they're bi. I didn't. It took me a lot of exploration, therapy, and self-reflection to realize and embrace my bisexuality. I recommend exploring your attractions without judgment and know that if you try something—like hooking up with a guy—and you don't like it, that doesn't make you any less straight.

How I wish I responded: The same way.

The second way this question is asked usually comes from a straight or gay person who wants to somehow "prove" I'm not bisexual. Some monosexuals take a perverse glee in trying to illustrate that I, a proud bisexual person, am somehow not bisexual. They try to trap me in a "gotcha" moment. They're waiting for my response, so they can say, "Actually, that just means you're gay!"

---

*The New York *Daily News* really did call me that, and you better believe I'm putting it on my tombstone.

How I've responded: I like dating and hooking up with guys, girls, and everyone in between, so that seems pretty bisexual to me.

How I wish I responded: How did you know you're straight, you punk-ass bitch?

But when's the last time you had sex with a woman?

This is another attempted trap to prove that I'm not bisexual. The naysayers believe that if I haven't slept with a woman recently, that means I'm no longer bi. Not true! Some bi people have never slept with the same sex or gender, and they're still bisexual. Bisexuality is about attractions, not behavior. That's why monogamous people are still bisexual despite the fact they're only sleeping with one person. That's why virgins can still be bisexual, gay, or straight.

While the assumption has always been that bi men are actually just gay, this is beginning to change. More recently, I've seen an emerging group of white, cisgender, heterosexual men who have erroneously said they're fluid, bisexual, pansexual, or queer as an odd form of oppression chasing. They claim a bi identity because they haven't come to terms with their many privileges and feel like there's clout in being marginalized. Because, yes, ask any marginalized person about the many perks of being societally (or governmentally) marginalized . . .

Being open to kissing a man or down with having an MFM three-some with another dude as long as your dicks don't touch doesn't make you bi. I'm 100 percent going to gate-keep your ass. You, sir, are not a faggot. Countless women have made out with other women, and they don't claim they're bi. They're just not homophobic; it's a fucking kiss! Are you attracted to men? Are you open to dating men? Are you going to suck my dick? Will you at least let me suck yours? If not, fuck off!

You're just a straight dude who's not homophobic, and you don't get to claim that you're queer. Embrace being straight. Let us pine after you! It's okay—we can still be friends.

How I've responded: I'm not proud to admit this, but when I've been asked in the past, I've validated their question by sharing the last time I had sex with a woman. (It's always recent because I'm constantly having sex with everyone of all genders.)

How I wish I responded: I'm fucking your mom.

How I wish I responded (option 2): You know, I'd still be bisexual even if I hadn't had sex with a woman in the past year—even if I'd never had sex with a woman. But since you asked nicely, I'll tell you: I'm fucking your mom.

I don't think I could date a bi man.

Um . . . I was not asking to date you. You don't go up to a Black person and out of thin air say, "I don't think I could ever date a Black person." That would be weird, inappropriate, and racist.

Still, I don't think it's necessarily biphobic if you're unwilling to date a bi person. If you're not willing to date a bi guy because *he sucks dicks, that's gross, and I don't want none of that gay shit*—yeah, that's pretty biphobic. But if you are someone who's deeply insecure and can't shake your fear that I, a bi man, am going to leave you for a person of another gender, I applaud you for knowing that about yourself. I'd rather you say "I'm not secure in myself to date a bi man" than attempt to date me and subsequently be possessive, jealous, and untrusting.

How I've responded: Okay.

How I wish I responded: Okay.

I also used to be bisexual, but then I came out as gay.

No, you once *identified* as bisexual because you thought it was more palatable than being "full-blown gay." (It's not, by the way.) This statement isn't as innocuous as simply sharing your own sexual journey. No, he's pulling some sneaky shit. He is essentially saying, "Bisexuality was a stepping-stone for me, and I believe it is one for you, too."

How I've responded: Well, I'm bisexual and plan to remain bisexual.

How I wish I responded: Well, I'm bisexual and plan to remain bisexual.

Bisexuality doesn't exist in men.

I'm sorry, but my identity, my sexuality, and how I go through the world is not up for debate. A few years ago, I would have indulged this game by listing all the men, women, and nonbinary people I've fucked, but I don't do that anymore. (That list is too long, and I got places to be; there's a guy 1,850 feet away who's waiting for me facedown, ass up.) You not believing in bisexuality doesn't make it any less real or make me any less bisexual. You can bury your head in the sand and pretend something doesn't exist, but that doesn't make it go away. And guess what? I don't need your approval. I know I'm bisexual whether you believe me or not.

How I responded (in my early twenties): Bisexuality obviously exists in men. I'm bisexual. I'm attracted to men, women, and all other genders. It's really offensive that you think that [and then proceed to ramble].

How I respond now: Okay.

I cannot emphasize enough how powerful it is when you don't take the bait. Not just to this particular comment, but to all comments that demand you to defend who you are. It illustrates that you don't care what they think. Their opinion doesn't matter, and you are so steadfast in your beliefs, so sure of who you are, that you don't require their support or approval. Ironically, not engaging is actually going to make them *more* likely to change their mind than a coherent, well-executed argument.

Are you equally attracted to men and women?

First and foremost, this question excludes nonbinary people. The correct way to ask this question is, "Are you equally attracted to all genders?" The short answer is: I don't know. The long answer is: There is so much that goes into attraction that it's challenging to quantify and parse out. Compared to other bi and pan people I know, I seem to be more equally attracted to all genders, at least if you're looking at my body count, which I don't recommend. While I really don't have a preference for a specific gender, I can tell you that regardless of gender, I know what I'm attracted to: I like 'em thicc, whether that be your breasts, your ass, your dick, or your arms. (Yes, I know, my attractions are a tad bit basic.)

However, when I sleep with a ton of men, I notice that I miss sleeping with women, and when I'm sleeping with lots of women, I miss men. When I haven't slept with trans/nonbinary people, I miss them, and when I haven't boned a goth, self-proclaimed bimbo, or short king, I miss them, too. Essentially I'm missing everyone all the time.

I don't think about this question often because I don't glean anything from the answer. Let's say I am slightly more attracted to women than men—so what? The only pertinent thing is if I find *you* attractive. It doesn't matter if I'm typically attracted to another gender more; what matters is I want to jump your bones here and now.

How I've responded: I'm pretty fifty-fifty, though sometimes I find myself more attracted to men and other times more attracted to women.

How I wish I responded: I'm not sure, but what I do know is I wanna fuck *you*.

What's the difference between dating men and women?*

This is one of those times when it's necessary to distinguish between sex and gender. It's not about what's hanging between your legs (if anything). It is more about how "masculine" or "feminine" you are.

Let me give an example: I've previously struggled dating some women because they pride themselves on having exaggerated feminine traits to the point that I'd call these traits toxically feminine. They would proudly say things like "I'm overly emotional because I'm a woman." Being overemotional, to me, doesn't constitute "womanhood." These women often craved that I "be the man" in our relationship; I guess they wanted me to grill meat, build furniture, and always cover the bill. (I don't know how to turn on a grill, have never held a power tool, and while I'm at it, I am going to say I don't know how to pay a bill.) These hyper-femme women believe in a rigid gender binary in a way that I don't, and for these reasons, I do not like dating them.

---

*Again, another question that excludes nonbinary folks.

Similarly, I don't like dating a man who embodies toxically masculine traits. I don't want a boyfriend who will beat up a dude just because he flirted with me. What I want is to have a threesome, obviously.

I like dating a person of any gender who doesn't believe in gender roles and believes we are true equals, as *people*. Typically, this tends to be with nonbinary folks or other queer men because we exist together outside of typical, gendered relationship dynamics. When neither of us is "the woman" in the relationship, there are fewer expectations for who should be doing what. It's simpler to create a more egalitarian dynamic that works for me and my partner.*

How I've responded: It really depends on the person.

How I wish I responded: You *want* me to say bitches be crazy. And you know what? Bitches can be crazy, but you forget that anyone can be a bitch, regardless of their sex or gender. I've met some crazy-ass male bitches and some chill-ass female bitches.

Do you prefer to date men or women?†

This is a slightly different question than above, and I can offer a more concrete answer: men. First and foremost, I feel welcome in gay spaces with my boyfriend. I can't go to a gay bar with my girlfriend or to a gay sex party . . . or I could, but I don't think the clientele of said party would be welcoming of a heterosexually perceived couple in a

---

*Even when I date queer and bi women, we still end up falling into a more traditional, gendered dynamic, even when we both try not to. It is simply too ingrained in us.

†People *really* don't like to include nonbinary folks when asking questions about bisexuality.

space meant for queer people.* If I kiss my partner on the lips, we're perceived as the shitty straight couple who comes into a gay bar and co-opts that space. This sucks for me because I want to share these fun experiences with my partner.

Second, to be blunt: I hate when people think I'm straight. When I walk around holding hands with a woman, I pass as straight (until I open my mouth). It's why I've noticed I subconsciously dress "queerer" when I'm out with a woman, as if to show the world, "Hey, we fuck, but I'm still queer!"

Third, I like getting railed. Sometimes, pegging just doesn't cut it. I need a flesh-and-blood cock to ███████████████████ ████████████████████████████████████ ████████████████████████████████████ ████████████████████████████████████.

How I've responded: Men (and then I explain the above).

How I wish I responded: Same.

Isn't everyone a little bisexual?

Nope, but YOU definitely are. Straight and gay people who are confident in their sexuality aren't saying everyone's a little bi. It's usually people who are, themselves, curious. Often, the curiosity is so little and so fleeting, they aren't sure what to do with it. It seems aggressive to think: *I find a few women really attractive, so I'm going to post up at the Cubbyhole and see if I can snag some snatch.*

---

*See my earlier point about how challenging it is to be "visibly bi." Even if my girlfriend were also bi, we'd be perceived as a straight couple until we said—*bisexual audibility*—that we're queer.

How I've responded: No, but I wish everyone was.

How I wish I responded: No, but you might be.

That's hot.

Fuck it, fetishize me, but only if you're a woman! When gay men fetishize me, it often comes from a fetishization of masculinity—that my sleeping with a woman somehow makes me more of a "man." That's fucked-up. But if you're a woman and you find it hot that I fuck dudes, go for it. Just fuck me, too.

How I've responded: *Smiles seductively**

How I wish I responded: *Smiles seductively**

I feel like bisexuality is very hip right now.

By calling bisexuality "hip," you insinuate that it's temporary. After all, nothing stays hip forever. It also negates the very real, hard work that bi people—and queer people at large—are doing to be perceived as more than a fad or lifestyle. Bisexuality isn't a phase, and the greater number of folks identifying as such will retain their sexuality. They won't go back to being gay or straight when bisexuality is no longer "cool."

How I've responded: We're definitely seeing more people embrace their attractions to all genders.

How I wish I responded: Same.

Isn't everyone your age bisexual now?

No, we're not all bi. However, we are starting to identify as bisexual in greater numbers.

A 2015 study by YouGov that nearly broke the quinternet (queer internet) revealed that 29 percent of young Americans aged 18–24 don't identify as exclusively gay or straight. That number was nearly 50 percent for young men and women in the UK. The Brits are always ahead of the curve.

But it's not just younger Americans who are starting to embrace their attraction to multiple genders. In that same 2015 study, a total of 16 percent of people (of all ages) didn't identify as exclusively gay or straight. That number jumped to 20 percent when YouGov replicated the study in 2018. In other words, we are multiplying. Soon, we will take over the world. If only Pinky and the Brain were bisexual, they would have achieved world domination sooner. (Who am I kidding? They were 100 percent bisexual.)

While more people than ever are identifying as bisexual, this is not due to a change in genetics or hormones in the milk. Rather, bisexuality is becoming more accepted as rampant homophobia/biphobia decreases globally. More people are publicly embracing the fact they are bi. But bisexuality existed well before droves of Millennials started claiming the label. There have always been men, women, and nonbinary folks who like getting down with all genders.

How I've responded: We're definitely seeing more people embrace their attractions to all genders.

How I wish I responded: Isn't everyone your age useless?

What's the difference between having sex with men and having sex with women?

This is an interesting question, but for the zillionth time, one that's exclusionary of nonbinary folks, so I'm not a huge fan of it. Nevertheless, there are big differences, most of which are learned and not innate. In my experience, both cis and trans men tend to be more aggressive and sure of what they want in bed. If I ask, "What do you want me to do?" they know and tell me. I think it's because I'm sleeping with queer men and not straight men, and we're accustomed to sharing our sexual preferences (e.g., top and bottom). Additionally, we tell no fewer than five different men a day on Sniffies what we're into (with graphic detail and illustrations).

Now many of the cis women I've slept with don't know how to answer that question. Or they seem more reluctant to reveal their desires. I often get responses of "What you're doing is fine!" or "Whatever you want." I know these responses are often due to women being conditioned to suppress their sexuality or being taught that their pleasure is secondary to the man's. Regardless, that makes sex less enjoyable for me—and presumably for her, too. Still, I've noticed that bisexual and polyamorous women tend to be more dominant and vocal about what they want sexually. I'm very much here for that.

The transgender/nonbinary folks I've hooked up with tend to be more sure of what they want sexually, too. This is likely due to trans/NB folks being a part of the queer community, which tends to more openly discuss sex. Additionally, in my experience, trans and NB folks tend to focus less on P-in-V or P-in-B penetration, focusing more on pleasure. Something we all should do regardless of gender or sexual orientation!

How I've responded: Some shorter version of what I expressed.

How I wish I responded: Same as above.

I've never met a bisexual person.

Ah, you've never met an *out* bisexual person. There is quite a difference, my friend. As far as responses on this list go, I don't hate this one. I feel like it's an opportunity to teach about bisexuality, since the person is often coming from a place of interest or intrigue. And I've made a career out of teaching people about bisexuality—this is my time to shine!

How I've responded: You've never met an *out* bisexual person, but I'm sure you've met plenty of bi people. Bi people tend to not be out the same way as gay folks because people assume a lot of hurtful and negative stereotypes about bi people.

How I wish I responded: Same as above!

Bisexuality is transphobic.

I've heard this from queer Gen-Zers and some younger Millennials. Their logic is such: Bisexuality has the prefix "bi," meaning "two," which refers to men and women. Therefore, it's exclusionary of trans people. This makes no fucking sense. Trans men are men, and trans women are women, so if you're making that distinction, I'd argue that you are the transphobic one. The argument to be made is that it's exclusionary of nonbinary people or anyone who doesn't identify as a man or woman.

Still, I think that's utterly ridiculous, a major reason being that the majority of self-identified bi people are indeed attracted to all genders. We use the word bi because that was the word we had. When bisexuality broke into modern vernacular, however many years ago, we didn't yet have the same language and nuanced understanding of gender that we have now. And from what I've gathered, bisexuality previously referred to biological sex and not gender. In this regard, it was actually inclusive, as nonbinary people still have a biological sex (i.e., assigned female at birth or assigned male at birth).

So, I simply do not believe that whoever coined "bi" was like, "But exclude those nonbinary people. I don't wanna fuck them!"*

Of note, the people who typically claim that being bisexual is transphobic are not trans or nonbinary themselves. They're cisgender people getting offended on behalf of a population who are not offended themselves. Do you know why trans or nonbinary people (typically) do not believe that bisexuality is exclusionary? Because bi people are the ones dating and fucking them! Do you think the toxically masculine straight dude is openly dating a nonbinary person? No, we are, by a large proportion.

How I've responded: Honestly, I get pretty upset and should work on not letting my anger lead this discussion. I just find it absurd that the vast majority of straight, cis men wouldn't openly date a trans woman, yet bi people who date and love trans/nonbinary folks are deemed transphobic. One of my least favorite things is when progressives cannibalize each other, which is what's happening!

---

*Actually, we do know a little bit about the history of the word "bisexual." Before it was used to discuss attraction, bisexuality described having both male and female reproductive organs. In humans, many now call this being intersex. However, bisexual is still used among botanists to describe plants that have male and female reproductive organs within the same flower. Bisexual was then used to describe folks who embodied both traditionally masculine and feminine characteristics—androgynous folks—many of whom would likely identify as nonbinary today. It really wasn't until the 1970s that our current definition of bisexuality, as a sexual orientation indicating attraction, became the more commonly used definition.

How I wish I responded: Taking a step-by-step approach, explaining the history of bisexuality, why it's not transphobic, and how we (pansexuals, bisexuals, fluid folks, etc.) have very similar sexual orientations. We should unite instead of picking each other apart.

Oh, I identify as pansexual.

Notice the "Oh." This has happened a few times, and I really get the vibe that pansexuals feel like they're out-woke-ing and one-upping bisexuals. I'm attracted to all genders, so my attractions fit pansexuality (or at least one definition of pansexuality). But there are reasons why I proudly claim bi as opposed to pan.

First, I didn't know about the other labels when I thought I might also be attracted to genders other than women. When I discovered the label, it fit. When I embraced it, I felt part of the LGBTQ community. For the first time, I knew who I was. By the time I learned of these other labels, I had grown attached to bisexuality and have had no desire to abandon it.

Second, I claim bisexuality for visibility. I want folks to avoid the trouble I went through as a teenager and young adult. I want kids questioning their sexuality to see that we exist, are real, diverse, and proud. We're not confused. Do you know how kids and adults find my work? Through Google. So now this is a matter of SEO (search engine optimization). If I claimed pansexual, people who don't know that word wouldn't find me when they Googled me. Bisexuality has a long history of usage and understanding, so it's a word I want to keep using.

Third, I claim it to honor the great bi people who came before me, including the LGBTQ activists and trans icons Sylvia Rivera and Marsha P. Johnson.

Lastly, I claim it for community. The term bisexual is an inclusive identity, a historical identity, and one that all people attracted to more than one gender can rally behind.

I hope this doesn't come off as panphobic or discouraging of non-monosexual neopronouns (such as omnisexual, multisexual, polysexual, and ambisexual). I want you to identify with whatever label you think fits you best. I simply would like you to extend that same courtesy to me. I don't want to feel like my identity is somehow outdated, ignorant, or non-progressive. My identity is my identity, period.

How I've responded: I'm attracted to all genders but identify as bisexual.

How I wish I responded: Same.

But that's just because you're single. You'll functionally end up being gay or straight depending on who you settle down with.

To be fair, I've only heard this from my mom, and it's not coming from a place of bi-erasure. She simply wants me to "settle down" and give her grandbabies. She knows that my lifestyle isn't the most conducive to having rugrats.

How I've responded: I will still be bisexual even then.

How I wish I responded: You have two other straight sons who are both older and married. Why are you hitching yourself to my wagon?

Why should I come out as bi when I'm married and monogamous?

This often comes from bi folks who don't feel "queer" enough to claim the bi label. A cisgender woman married to a straight cis man hasn't experienced the same level of prejudice as a femme, gay man who's in a relationship with a nonbinary individual. However, your experience with oppression doesn't validate your queerness. How sad is it that our understanding of queer identity is inextricably linked to and dependent on having experienced oppression? Being queer is about your sexual and romantic attractions. It's about community. You're not queerer if you've been a victim of a hate crime.

And no (or few) cis, bisexual women who are happily and monogamously married are saying that they've experienced the same level of hardships as trans and nonbinary people. But that doesn't make them any less queer. It doesn't mean they can't claim bisexuality.

There's power in numbers, and having more bi people in the LGBTQ community allows for more activism. For example, might a monogamous bi woman be more likely to use her husband's investment banker money to donate to LGBTQ organizations if she feels like she's truly a member of the LGBTQ community? If she feels ostracized by queers, she's not going to open her purse.

How I've responded: You are queer enough. We need more bisexual visibility. Please come out and be a member of the LGBTQ community!

How I wish I responded: The same, just louder!

Do you want kids?

This literally has nothing to do with bisexuality, but I don't like this question, so I figured I'd throw it in.

How I've responded: Not for the foreseeable future.

How I wish I responded: Mom, seriously, you need to stop.

X X X

Here's the thing about unlearning what society teaches you: You still live in that society. While you may be more open, or dare I say enlightened, most people are not. So you spend your life in opposition to the majority opinion, and you have to learn how to interact with everyone else in a manner that doesn't drive you completely bonkers.

You may not believe all the negative stereotypes about bisexuality, but others do. While I used bisexuality to illustrate my point, you can easily substitute other concepts that render similar suspicion and confusion, such as "polyamory," "kink," and even "feminism." People have equally distorted ideas about these lifestyles and ideologies.

It's necessary to learn how and when it's worth engaging, and when it's simply too much. It took me a long time to open up about my bisexuality with strangers. It took me an even longer time to learn how to respond and when to sit quietly. Remember, you don't need someone you just met or a stranger online to validate any aspect of your identity. You are still bi when they say bisexuality isn't real. You are still trans when they purposefully misgender and deadname you. And you're still a Boyslut even if you haven't gotten gonorrhea in the past year.

CHAPTER 9

IS THIS HOW I DIE?

His first message got my attention: "My door will be unlocked. I'll be blindfolded and tied up to the bed with my head over the side. Come in, facefuck me, and go." He then shared his location. No more than an eight-minute walk from my humble abode in Somerville, Massachusetts.

I wanted to go over—of course I did. This sounded hot as fuck, and I famously *love* a good facefucking. But I was new to Grindr. I had only hooked up with two guys from the app beforehand with limited success. The first guy was fifteen years older and fifty pounds heavier than he was in the photos he sent. (We still had sex.) I couldn't get hard with the second guy because I was a nervous wreck. Or rather, I kept losing my erection whenever I went to put on a condom.

This third potential meeting piqued my interest. I knew I'd be able to perform because I wouldn't feel any pressure. He was blind-folded and couldn't see me. If I couldn't get hard, I could pull up my pants and be out his door within seconds. No awkward conversation about my ED.

But it also sounded so aggressive. *How on Earth is he saying that to a random stranger on the internet? Leaving his door unlocked while he's tied up? I could just rob him. Wait, how is he tying* himself *up?*

During my early days on Grindr, the whole premise seemed bananas. I found it inconceivable to hop online, have a stranger to your door in seven minutes, fuck him for seven minutes, and then: poof, gone! I couldn't tell you the number of times a guy came over while my roommate was cooking dinner and left before my roommate had started eating.

"Hi, great to meet you," Evan would say, stirring whatever was in the wok.

"Hope you had fun," he'd say nine minutes later, stirring the same wok.

I was also bewildered by how immediately and directly you could look for sex. No small talk, no discussion of how your day went or what you thought of last night's *Drag Race* elimination. Grindr was simple: a hole pic and a location.

This was a strange new world unlike any of my experiences with women. I'm not saying that women aren't down to have casual sex, but I've never had a Tinder match send me an unsolicited pic of her vulva with an address in tow before we recapped our weeks.

While I appreciated the direct, no-nonsense approach to casual sex, it also scared the living bejeezus out of me. I'd been taught not to talk to strangers, let alone step into their van to delight in their candy. Grindr quickly had me talking to strangers and tasting their butterfingers. (Or buttering my fingers.) It did not seem safe. Not one bit. But that's what made it so fucking hot.

I ended up walking over to the open-throated man, a mere 0.4 mile from my apartment. In that brief walk along the Minuteman Bikeway, I had only one thought: *Is this how I die?* I then imagined how devastated my mom would be and how embarrassed she'd be to tell her friends. How could she explain that her son Dickarus had flown too close to the sun-tanned bussy?

We've established that I'm neurotic, but Grindr murderers are a thing! In fact, I was meeting this kinky man during the heyday of Stephen Port, aka the Grindr Killer. On the other side of the pond, the British serial rapist and killer used Grindr to lure men to his flat, where he would drug them with GHB and then proceed to rape and murder them.*

You would think I would have turned around. You would think the innate evolutionary urge to protect myself from death would have kicked in. But another evolutionary urge took precedence: blood rushing to my dick. I was hard as a rock on the way over. Apparently, fear of death can be a powerful aphrodisiac.

To be fair, I didn't *really* think I was going to die. It was a concern, but I also had countless gay friends who used the app, and none of them ended up in a tub full of blood—at least not without consenting. Back in 2015, Grindr had already assumed some cultural prominence, no longer an up-and-coming app only a handful of men used. It was a phenomenon that countless young, queer men enjoyed (and loathed).

I facefucked him, in case you were wondering. His door was unlocked, and he lay on his back, blindfolded, just as he had promised. I didn't say anything upon arriving. Neither did he. I simply tightened his restraints so he could not move, dropped my sweats, and went to town on his throat. It was awesome.

X X X

While Grindr always piqued my interest, I had refrained for years. It all seemed too intense. Eventually, my aggressively straight friend Robert convinced me to download the second-most-addictive app in the world—the first being Candy Crush, obviously.

"Do you know how much I would kill for a straight version of Grindr?" Robert asked.

---

*Port is currently serving a "whole life order" in prison, the English equivalent of a life sentence without the possibility of parole.

"Isn't that Tinder?"

"No, you know it's not. I still have to take girls out on Tinder. I'm not sending nudes to her. I'm not going over to her house, fucking her, and then never speaking to her again."

"I guess so," I replied.

"But you can! You like guys and girls. Guys are easy. Go fuck them."

"I don't know," I said.

"Come on! This is a no-brainer. You get to fuck a ton of dudes. Do it for me, man, since I can't. Go make me jealous."

Reluctantly I downloaded it, and Robert quickly regretted turning me on to the bussy buffet. We used to hang out a few times a week after work, but the moment I downloaded Grindr, I abandoned him for three months. Eventually, he called me out.

"Dude, where have you been? What have you been doing?" he asked.

"I have fucked, like, fifty guys."

"Wait, what?" he said. Before I downloaded Grindr I had fucked a total of two men, which Robert knew.

Robert lost it. He was in utter disbelief. "Are you serious? That's fucking insane! Holy shit! What's happened?"

I pulled up the app and showed him *exactly* what happened. He had only ever heard stories about the interface, and while he knew it was easy to fuck men, he didn't realize it was *so* easy to fuck men. A few men messaged me when I logged on. I said what's up and sent nudes. They replied with nudes. I asked them where they were and ping: an address.

He was in shock that I set up multiple fucks within a minute. "Wait, so are you going to fuck them?"

"No, I'm at work."

"So you're just going to leave them hanging?"

"It's Grindr, everyone flakes all the time. No one gives a fuck."*

I proceeded to tell Robert about a few of my wilder hookups, including the open-throated man. With each story, his jaw dropped slightly further.

Was I ever afraid, he wanted to know? Initially, yes, but with each successful hookup that ended in an orgasm and not a decapitation, I became less worried, to the point where my fear was nearly gone.

I'll also acknowledge that I'm six-four and 185 pounds, so I'm not exactly the first pick of a guy to overpower physically. While I take zero safety precautions whatsoever—I simply hope that I've done enough good in this world that karma will protect me—I understand not everyone is so safe or privileged. And certainly there are ways to use the app safely—tell your friends where you're going, meet in a public place first, maybe even ask to FaceTime to get a vibe check . . . though there are some seriously charming serial killers out there.

It's bewildering how theoretically unsafe Grindr is, yet how safe it seems to be in practice. While I've heard a handful of stories of abuse and violence, they happen a fraction of the time. Considering how often meetings take place through Grindr, tens of thousands of men meeting across the globe daily, you would expect to hear more horror stories.

While safety isn't as large of a concern as one would expect, there are still approximately one million issues that have arisen since the app's birth in 2009. Ones that affect all queer men regardless of whether they use the app or not.

Second only to PrEP, I believe Grindr has had the most significant impact on queer men and gay male culture in the past two decades. The legalization of same-sex marriage in the United States pales in impact when compared to the monolith that is Grindr. Sure, same-

*That first sentiment was true. The second, not so much. I'm no longer a flake now, though. I promise!

sex marriage gave us some rights and was a symbol of LGBTQ progress, but it only affects queer men and women who want to marry a same-sex partner (which isn't most of us). A 2021 Gallup poll showed that fewer than 10 percent of adult LGBTQ Americans are married to a same-sex spouse. I can sure as hell tell you there are a LOT more men using Grindr (or Scruff, or Sniffies, or Jack'd) than getting married—not to mention all the married men on Grindr, whom I know intimately.

So what, exactly, has Grindr done besides give me multiple anal fissures and the clap repeatedly? How, exactly, has it changed how queer men interact, love, and fuck beyond upping everyone's body count tenfold? (Spoiler: It's not all rainbows, butterflies, and open throats. It's harmed us in numerous ways, too.)

It's made finding sex so much easier.

You don't have to leave your apartment to find sex. You don't need to go to a gay bar. You don't need to cruise at the park. You simply need to hop on your phone to find a guy nearby who's down to fuck. You might be thinking, "Zach, it's not that easy for the rest of us out there who aren't traditionally attractive and six-four." To this I say, bullshit. Sure, you might not have as easy of a time as other folks, but I literally fuck the closest person to me, no matter how they look, because when I'm on Grindr, I'm not on looking for love. I'm there with a singular purpose: getting my dick wet. And I know there are plenty of guys like me who aren't prioritizing physical attraction when they're scrolling through Grindr. They just want sex and love the anonymity of it. They love how primal it is. So yes, I believe you, or even a literal goblin, can find casual sex on Grindr.

Perpetually having access to sex at your fingertips is a double-edged sword, though. It's great when you're home alone, bored, and horny. It's bad, well, every other time. There have been months in my life where I really wanted a boyfriend, but instead of asking guys on official dates, I would hop on Grindr, find the nearest boy, and invite him over for sex. It was just *easier* than going on a date. I didn't want to have to get dressed up, take a train into town, and discuss all the boring first date questions. I wanted to smoke weed and cum. The thing is, I deluded myself into thinking that I was going to find a boyfriend on Grindr, but cumming and leaving isn't exactly conducive to emotional intimacy.

A gay man looking for love on Grindr is like a dude going to a butcher shop to find fruit. Sure, they may have an apple available for purchase—maybe to put in the pig's mouth—but if you're looking for fruit, go to a farmer's market.

Similarly, if you're looking for love, use Bumble or Hinge—apps that cater to committed romantic relationships. I have a couple of gay friends who lament the seeming ubiquity of open relationships. Well, yes, because they're talking to men on *Grindr*, an app for casual sex. I know I keep belaboring this, but my God, stop pretending hookup apps are the best way to find a boyfriend!

Now let's say you're someone who's good about going on dates. You only use Grindr to scratch that sexual itch when you have nothing better to do, but since you're looking for love, you still meet men IRL or use relationship apps. Good job! That isn't a simple feat. But are you using Grindr at inopportune times? When you're with your friends, do you hop on it just to see who's in the area? When you're on a date, do you find yourself checking it when you're in the bathroom? When you're on a strict deadline, are you futzing around on Grindr instead? I had to make a rule for myself that I would only check Grindr when I was alone (or when I'm with my partner and we're looking for a third). It's so easy to get distracted and lost in all the buttholes on Grindr. Before you know it, you've been on it for an hour, and still no one is interested. That's when it's time to cut your losses and jerk off.

A 2017 study conducted by the website Time Well Spent surveyed two hundred thousand iPhone users by tracking their time on-screen and then asking how much of that time was spent happy or unhappy. With 77 percent of users leaving the app feeling unhappy, Grindr was ranked number one for unhappiest app. Those who said Grindr left them feeling unhappy tended to use the app for more than an hour a day. There's a lesson here. Personally, if no one is en route after fifteen minutes in Grindrville, I log off, pet the one-eyed snake, and head to bed. (Adulting, baby!)

It's made cheating so much easier.

This is because Grindr gives you unfiltered access to an unlimited supply of horny dudes mere feet away. I can't prove this, but if I had to bet, I'd say most gay/bi men cheat on their partner with a guy they met on a hookup app. I believe this based on the questions I receive for Sexplain It, as well as from my "monogamous" friends. It's just so easy to send nudes to a guy nearby. You tell yourself, "Oh I'd never actually fuck them, I just like sending and receiving nudes," but bitch, be real. You want to fuck and one drunk night, you just might.

Does your husband know you have a Grindr where you solicit nudes? No, he'd be furious if he found out, so you're keeping it a secret from him? That is cheating. Sure, you're not balls deep in some twink, but that still constitutes cheating!

I've come to realize that when a guy on Grindr asks me to wear a condom, it's usually because he's cheating. At first I thought he took one look at me and knew I was a walking STI, but nope. He's wrapping it up because giving your partner the drip is a surefire way to let him know that you haven't been faithful.

The anonymity and virtual distance of Grindr facilitates cruelty and enables all the social isms and phobias.

Before delving into this point, I want to acknowledge that I am a tall, white, muscular, cisgender, masculine-presenting, HIV-negative man. I haven't experienced much fat-phobia, racism, transphobia, femme-phobia, or HIV-shaming on the app. Still, I think it's necessary to discuss these issues. Frankly, it would be obtuse not to address them when examining the impact of Grindr on the queer community.

There have been countless social psychology studies that have illustrated that anonymity makes people cruel. Frankly, it's obvious. You're (hopefully) an adult; you've been on the internet. People feel emboldened and empowered to be their worst selves from the safety of their toilet seat. So this isn't just a "gay" or "queer" thing. Generally speaking, a certain subset of the population will be unnecessarily mean and hostile online regardless of sexual orientation. (I was going to say regardless of gender or sexual orientation, but I've found that men are significantly worse than women.)

Trolls and assholes on Grindr aren't happy because happy men don't attack strangers online for no goddamn reason. They are definitely dealing with unresolved issues, and I extend them some empathy. While you'd think being bullied, rejected, and identifying as part of a minority group under the queer rainbow would make you more compassionate—alas, the opposite is often true. Similarly, you would think that gays bullied for something they cannot control would be kinder to the plights of people of color, who similarly did not choose their race. Yet again, you'd be wrong. It turns out white gay men are still white men.

There's a staggering amount of racist behavior happening on Grindr. There's also a lot of racism masquerading as "preferences." I understand that we can't force attraction—ask any gay man who's tried forcing heterosexuality. However, there are two things we can control that, to me, separate racism and preferences. The first, simply, is an openness. While you may not typically be attracted to, say, Asian men, you shouldn't rule out every Asian man on the planet before getting to know them. Saying you're not attracted to someone solely because of their race before you've even met them is racist.

Fun fact, I used to not be "into" plus-sized guys (but I was never a dick about it). However, there were a couple of bigger guys I found myself attracted to (I was open), so we fucked, and guess what? I loved it. Turns out big guys have big asses—and I love me a big, juicy ass. My openness didn't just lead me to fun and new sexual experiences, it was also a differentiating act between me being fat-phobic and not.

Even though you can't control your attractions, you can control your response—and that, to me, is the second factor that separates preferences from racism. For example, you don't have to tell someone you're not interested in their entire race as a response to a "hi" from a rando hottie on Grindr. You can simply say, "You're super cute, but I'm not looking." (Notice how I didn't say "my type," which is just a thinly veiled code for race.) Conversely, you could not respond. It's free! It's easy! It takes no effort at all! Your mom had it right—if you don't have anything nice to say . . . Well, that holds true with Grindr, too. You don't have to reply to everyone who sends you an unsolicited pic of their butthole.

Prejudice on Grindr—and its ensuing cringe-worthy messages and responses—isn't just limited to race. There's all sorts of othering happening, from body shaming to straight-up internalized homophobia. (Log onto Grindr and see if you can find a profile on your grid that doesn't say "no femmes." It's harder than you'd think.) There's also transphobia and HIV-shaming—really, these self-hating bigots take *any* opportunity to reject, other, and belittle members of their own community.

All of this is to say, dudes are unnecessarily brutal when rejecting guys on hookup apps; if Grindr has done anything, it's revealed and even normalized how racist, fat-phobic, femme-phobic, transphobic, and HIV-phobic the queer community can be.

We, as a community, need to do better. My God! Being kind doesn't cost you a dime, and it's okay to be nice to someone even if you don't want to fuck them. I know you're dealing with your issues—we all are—but at the very least, let's not project our insecurities and struggles onto others. And let's not be assholes to someone because they're different from us—you know, *exactly* what we ask of straight people.

It's increased how often we're (brutally) rejected.

As much as I've tried, I don't think I've completely solved the world's social and race issues in my last seven hundred words. I also don't think I've made every cruel man kinder. Men have been and will continue to be needlessly hurtful while rejecting. Or they'll say they're on their way, so you take the time to douche. After an hour of waiting, you text, "What's your ETA?" only to get blocked.

I've talked about how painful rejection can be, and even knowing this we still log onto an app where we get rejected like it's our goddamn job. I'd say I get a response from about a quarter of the men I message first on Grindr. Some don't see my messages, but most leave me on read.

While getting rejected online isn't the same as getting rejected IRL, it still hurts. There's also a higher probability of rejection—more messages mean more chances to have a door shut in your face. Quantifying the pain of rejection isn't possible, but I'm going to do it anyway! Let's say you getting rejected online is a quarter as painful as getting rejected IRL. When you're out, you may get rejected by two guys. However, when you're online, you'll likely get rejected by (or no response from) twenty-five guys. The sheer number of rejections is overwhelming online, and while individually they may not be *that* bad, that pain accumulates over time.

These rejections make us question ourselves. We think that we must be a "certain type of gay" to get laid. We begin to hate our bodies or our skin color. We question whether we should present more masculine, even if that's not who we really are. We begin to think we're unfuck-able, unlovable, and doomed to spend the rest of our lives alone. The fucked-up thing is that we're right. Well, no, we're definitely fuckable and lovable. But I mean that if you were a white, masculine dude with negative 4 percent body fat, you would get more responses. I'm not going to pretend otherwise.

But there is some good news. You can message ten guys/trans women/nonbinary folks and if only one responds, comes over, and you have a blast together, that's all you need. (Unless you were looking for a threesome, then better luck next time.)

When I get rejected cruelly on Grindr, I try not to internalize whatever bullshit they said. I (attempt) to be grateful they showed their true colors from the get-go. It's gratifying to not sleep with a massive dick. Massive dicks hurt anyway! No time wasted, and on an app whose secondary function is to seemingly waste time, that's a good thing.

I once had a guy come over and say I didn't look like my pictures and that he wasn't into me. He then turned around and left. How dare he because I look exactly like my pictures. I am not a catfish. Don't gaslight me! That encounter stung. As good as I am at getting rejected, that felt really shitty. But hey, it was for the better because I never want to sleep with anyone who doesn't want to sleep with me. None of us should, and we shouldn't pine after these men either.

Now if you're someone who *only* messages the classically attractive dom tops with arms the size of footballs and abs you can grate cheese on, and proceed to complain about how they don't respond, that's on you. You gotta be a little bit more open to different types of men. See what happens, that's all I'm saying.

It's increased opportunities for fetishization.

On the opposite side of the spectrum of rejection is fetishization, which, ironically, can feel worse than rejection. Fetishization runs rampant on gay hookup apps, largely because guys don't understand that it's a problem. They think they're complimenting someone. While compliments are good, fetishizing is not!

A question I'm often asked, and one I love answering: How do I know when my attractions cross the line and become a fetish? I find it interesting that certain fetishes are completely acceptable. For example, I undeniably have a fetish for big, juicy asses. You've probably gathered this by now. You should see my Instagram feed: It's just one bubble butt after another. This fetish seems pretty tame and unprejudiced because almost anyone can have a big ass. A big, juicy ass knows no single race, gender, or sexual orientation. Aliens, I presume, can have big, juicy asses.

Still, I have taken my fetish too far at times. This happened when a person stopped being a person and was just an ass. When I was in my early twenties, whenever I saved a Grindr fuck's contact to my phone, I would use their ass pic as the contact photo. So I would save a number as "Jay Gri," and when he texted me, his juicy booty in a jockstrap would pop up above his message. An hour later, he'd be facedown, ass-up in my bed, which was fine by me since I couldn't remember what his face looked like anyway.

All things considered, my fetish was pretty harmless. They never knew that's how I saved their contact info (until now), and when they came over, we had great sex where I did not solely focus on praising their ass.* All parties won, though I can't say this is exactly laudatory behavior.

But the difference between a healthy attraction and a fetish is similar to the difference between a preference and being racist. It's not actually the feelings or attractions as much as how you act on them. Because again, you can't help whom or what you're attracted to, but you can control what you say and do.

Let me break down a more personal example. I fucking LOVE having sex with trans women. Big fake tits and a dick? Hot. Great. Ten out of ten recommend. But when talking to a trans woman or having sex with a trans woman, I don't mention their dick at all. I don't even touch it unless she wants me to because touching or commenting on her dick can be triggering, as it can cause major gender dysphoria. So, I simply enjoy looking at it and getting turned on by it. I also treat her like an entire person and do not reduce her to a single aspect of her body. That's because she *is* a whole human being and not just the sum of her parts. (I know! Wild, right?)

Let's say you're into Black guys and aren't sure whether your attractions border on a fetish. When you are talking to or fucking a Black guy, are you commenting on their "chocolate skin"? Well, that's seeing him for a sum of one part: his skin. Are you commenting on their BBC (*not* the British Broadcasting Company)? Given what I have said, could you see how this is fetishizing? That doesn't mean you can't enjoy his BBC. It doesn't mean that you can't think, "God, I love his big black cock." You can't control what you think, and we all know that "trying not to think about something" never works. Besides, I'm not

---

*Then there were the times where they specifically wanted me to praise and solely focus on their ass. I felt like I was getting away with murder, when really, I was simply lucky to find someone with very compatible sexual desires.

the thought police. However, you can control what you say. So what you say is, "I love how your thick cock feels in my ass." That's still hot, right? I'm not THAT big of a buzzkill.

Grindr offers mini-bits of validation.

While the amount of validation we get on Grindr pales in comparison to the amount of rejection, fetishization, and vitriol we receive, we still crave those sweet little hits of dopamine. Getting validated from a headless torso, even if it's a simple "You're so hot," is, simply put, *nice*.

Validation is important—both internal and external. I'm seeing social media "empowerists" share things like, "You don't need validation from others. You just need to know your own worth and love yourself. All the validation you need can come from within."

A charming idea, but I'm not convinced. There are the select enlightened few who forgo all human pleasures and pains by becoming a hermit in the woods. They meditate for hours, live off the land, and bathe naked in streams as salmon fly through the air. Good for them, but the rest of us live in what's called a SoCiETy. And in this SoCiETy, we interact with others. It is completely normal, healthy, and necessary to get validation from people we interact with. Think about it in a work context. You want to feel validated and appreciated by your boss and coworkers. In fact, studies show that validation is one of the biggest factors dictating whether a person likes their job. Why would it be any different for relationships or life in general?

However, we don't need validation from *everyone*, and therein lies the problem. You don't need validation from a random stranger online who's probably catfishing you. You don't need it from *any* stranger, no matter what social media would have you believe. Would it be nice to be validated by countless strangers, nonetheless? Sure, I mean that's why many of us are on Grindr, or online in general, but you don't *need* it from these people. You *do* need it from the people in your life, real people who have heads attached to their torsos, like your friends, lovers, family members, and colleagues. And yes, okay, those "empowerists" have a point: You need to validate yourself, too.

I think it's important to remind yourself that you have a top-shelf bussy. Your hips do not lie. And you can, and have, sucked the soul out of someone's dick. As I write this, he aimlessly roams the streets, a shell of a man, searching for someone who can suck dick like you. I want you to focus on that man's life you destroyed by being too damn good at head. That's the internal validation I'm talking about!

It's helped queer men find a community.

While I've really shat on Grindr—and when I say Grindr, know I also mean Scruff, Jack'd, and every other gay hookup app—I want to say Grindr isn't *all* bad. Grindr has indeed connected the gay/queer community. I think of the little baby gay in Alabama who isn't out to his family but can talk to and meet other gay men in his area. Is it ideal that a sixteen-year-old is using a sex app to connect with other gay men? No, but sadly, we live in an unideal world where that's the only option for many teens.

I enjoy gay bars and clubs, but many gays don't, and when you don't, it can be hard to meet other queers. Through Grindr, you can meet other introverts, gamers, sober guys, and the like. There are quite a few guys on Grindr who mention that their interests are anime and video games. I'm always like, "Yes, let's watch *Kakegurui* and play *Super Smash Bros.* Loser sucks the winner's dick!"*

I've also met kink-compatible partners on Grindr. I have some really weird shit that I'm into (keep reading), and I have met guys who

---

*Fun fact, the first time I ever sucked a penis was this exact scenario. We wagered a blow job on *Smash,* and the loser had to drop to his knees. Even though I won, I still sucked his dick. So really, we both won.

share my intense kinks. Fabulous! Visibility and recognition also help normalize kinks. You see what other wild things these guys are into, and you think: "Wow, my desire to get pissed on while being called a pathetic whore is pretty common, and all things considered, not that wild."

I'm constantly asked to piss on guys or piss in their mouth. Apparently, I'm talented because I can "give it to them straight from the tap." Anyway, it's nice to have these conversations online before you meet up instead of asking someone to piss in your mouth while ordering a third round of beers.

But do you know what? It's actually not that wild to ask a guy you met out if he would come home and pee in your mouth. Grindr did that, or at least was partially responsible. I can't give Grindr all the credit here. I'm pretty sure gay rights and no longer being able to get fired from your job for being gay have contributed. But I think Grindr pushed the needle forward and helped to normalize openly talking about gay sex. After sharing our kinks with literally hundreds if not thousands of men online, many of us now feel more comfortable talking about gay sex IRL.

I called up my sixtysomething-year-old guncle—my expert source—to ask how open gay guys were talking about sex when he was in his twenties and thirties. "It's not at all like it is today," he said. "There was always a small subset who were out, aggressive, and talking about gay sex, but it's much more widespread now." The fact that I'm his nephew has undoubtedly distorted his perception, but still!

In Cumclusion . . .

I said earlier that Grindr is second to PrEP when it comes to largest impact. I stand by that. However, there have been countless straight people in my life who had no idea what PrEP was until I informed them, but they all knew about Grindr. Grindr's cultural impact extends beyond the queer community. It's taken on a symbolic omnipresence, and it's a lens through which straights view gay/bi men. *They're all a bunch of whores!* I'm sorry, but no, we're all a bunch of *Boysluts*—get it fucking right.

Yet as much as straights may think they "understand" Grindr, they never will—simply because Grindr is very personal to each of the queers who waste countless hours on it. For better or worse, so much of how we view ourselves, our relationships, and our desires has been shaped by Grindr. And Grindr isn't going away. The app may not last forever, but Scruff, Sniffies, Jack'd, Hornet, Adam4Adam, Growler, or some new gay hookup app will surely take its place.

Since Grindr is here to stay, much like that hookup who lingers after what was supposed to be a quickie, we need to learn how to live with it. Grindr is like alcohol: best enjoyed in moderation. However, Grindr isn't exactly a tool I'd recommend for self-discipline. After all, Grindr is designed for addiction (at least in my opinion). All "social" apps are. And knowing exactly how many feet he is away from you is so damn tempting. Who among us cannot make time for a quick fifteen-minute sex break—squeezing him in both literally and metaphorically?

Grindr makes sex easy, which is both its greatest strength and greatest weakness. It means that it's great for things that are easy, like having a meaningless quickie.* But for things that aren't easy, like finding love, being vulnerable, and gaining self-worth, you're going to need more than Grindr. It cannot and will not provide any shortcuts because there are no shortcuts for these things. They require work that extends beyond sending a stranger an unsolicited picture of your hairy asshole—but also, please keep sending me unsolicited pics of your hairy asshole because I love 'em!

---

*I know that many queer men struggle with casual sex and quickies. However, these men typically aren't on Grindr, so I'm not talking about them.

CHAPTER 10

DON'T BE GAY, JUST SHOVE IT UP YOUR ASS

J enny was the first person I dated after coming out as bisexual. I was on OkCupid for about a month before I received a personalized six-hundred-word message from her about how she was exploring her gender identity and hoped, since I was bisexual, that I would still be attracted to her no matter how she presented. She also shared that she was recently diagnosed with HSV-2, was taking Valtrex daily as a suppressant, and had been struggling to find men who were open to having sex with her. She said that I seemed really open-minded in my profile and was hoping neither of these "issues" would scare me off.

She was right. I didn't care about how she presented or wherever she landed on her gender identity because she was hot. That bone structure wasn't going anywhere regardless of whether she identified as a man, woman, neither, or both. As for her genital herpes status? She was taking antiviral medications daily as a suppressant and was clearly mindful of any outbreaks, so it was unlikely that she would pass on the virus. So the decision was easy: Go on a date with her.

Sitting at the dive bar of her choosing, I learned that at twenty-two, she was already an experienced kinkster. Her *thing* was to find beefy straight guys and peg them while calling them a "faggot" and "homo." While I now think "that's hot," at the time I wasn't turned on, though I wasn't turned off either. I panicked. I figured I was way too inexperienced to date someone with her kink experience and worried I would never be able to satisfy her.

It didn't help that Jenny was a stone-cold bitch, and I'm saying this with nothing but love and admiration. Born and raised in one of the cool parts of London, Jenny only wore black. She was six feet tall with a septum ring and fiery eyes that could look into the depths of your soul. Her ass? Bubbly. Her tits? Perky. Her legs? For days. With her resting bitch face, she was always the least approachable woman at the bar. You just got the vibe she would bite your head off if you glanced in her direction.

You'd never know it by looking at her, but Jenny had social anxiety. And since she presented how she did, her words and behaviors were often interpreted as "bitchy." But boy, did I love her, and she loved me. She was brilliant, creative, and always added something insightful to any conversation. She was also the first woman I met who didn't fear my bisexuality. She wasn't worried that I was going to leave her for a man, or another woman for that matter. She wasn't worried that I was secretly gay, and even encouraged my more feminine qualities. This may have to do with the fact that she, too, was bisexual, but I also think that when I wore a crop top and sequins, and she wore a hoodie and basketball shorts, it affirmed Jenny's identity as a trans man. (Soon after we began dating, Jenny started identifying as a trans man but still preferred she/her pronouns.)

In a strange way, we had that special relationship between a gay guy and his straight girl BFF. We would discuss our *Drag Race* opinions, dance together at gay clubs, and talk about how hot that dude was—only our night would end with *us* having fantastic sex.

And the more I got to know her, the more I realized that she was a big softy underneath her badass shell. As for her kinks, after talking more with her, I realized they were tools she used to better explore and understand her gender identity. She knew she was a bombshell when presenting as a woman and enjoyed the privileges of being, in her words, "a hot chick." She said she wasn't ready to give that up yet, even though presenting as a woman exacerbated her gender dysphoria. But when she got to peg a man, she felt connected to her identity as a trans man. The experience of having a dick and being dominant was both validating and affirming.

Now while I wanted to affirm her all night long, I was facing two issues with her kinks. First, I *am* a faggot. I have sucked hundreds of dicks. And you know what? There has never been a dick I could not deepthroat. Am I bragging? Yes, because I am talented. (This doesn't permit you to send me unsolicited dick pics . . . unless you have a *really* pretty penis.)

I knew if Jenny called me a "faggot" during sex, it wouldn't cause psychological turmoil the way it did when she had sex with straight men. Calling me a "faggot" would just be stating a fact. Since Jenny got off on humiliating the straight boys, and I didn't find it humiliating to be queer, the kink quickly lost its appeal for both parties.

When I expressed this to Jenny, she told me not to worry. She would still love to get up in my ass. However, and this was the second and much larger issue: Back then, I didn't bottom! Not because I was this aggressive dom top or anything like that. I had tried bottoming once, and it went disastrously. I was drunk—big surprise—but at least I did it with a man whom I liked and trusted. I did not douche before the encounter, not that I even knew how. I did not prepare by eating light or taking fiber pills.* I didn't plan in any way, shape, or form, so once he made it inside my tight, *tight* butthole, I only had one thought: I am shitting on his dick.

Fun fact: The first time you have anal sex it *really* feels like you're shitting because pooping is the only thing your asshole has (probably) ever done up until this point. So every time they take their dick out of

---

*While you don't technically have to do either of these things, I really do as an anxious Jew with IBS.

you, you think you're pooping. Then it feels like they're pushing that poop back inside of you. This is all to say that it's a jarring experience your first time around. It also explains why I kept asking my top, "Did I shit?"

Each time he said, "No, you're good." Around the fifth time, I shouted: "I really think I shat this time!" He said, "If you shit, you shit. It's fine. Stop asking!" It turns out asking your lover if you're defecating on his most prized possession isn't a huge turn-on. Who knew?

No longer as worried about feces, I tried to relax but couldn't. I clenched for dear life. I also could not steady my breath, so I sounded like I was hyperventilating. While we did use lube, it was not nearly enough.*

The morning after the experience, I went to wipe. Not only did it hurt, but I was also bleeding. I had gotten fissures before (see earlier chapter about my over-wiping habit), so it wasn't *that* strange of a sight to behold, but it still surprised me. Looking at the bright red toilet paper, I said to myself, "You know what, Zach? You're a top, and that's okay."

Lord knows there's a top shortage; I was doing the Lord's work by keeping my tight hole off the market.

But when I told Jenny about my first and only bottoming experience, she was not having it. "So you haven't tried since then?" she asked with more than a hint of judgment.

"My only time," I replied.

"Zach, then you *have* to try again," she said. "It feels AMAZING when you do it right, but you did everything wrong your first time. You didn't use enough lube. You were drunk. You clenched. You didn't clean out and were anxious about that. You have to give it another try when you're doing things right! I really think you'll love it."

———————

*Now when I bottom, there's lube everywhere. My entire apartment becomes a Slip 'N Slide. Then we become little penguins and slide around on our bellies.

BOYSLUT

I couldn't argue against her logic, but I still wasn't sold. I really didn't like it that first time and didn't want to put myself through that awkward pain again. Sensing my reservation, she continued, "Try it by yourself while you're in the shower. Grab some lube and finger your hole. And make sure to be turned on while you're fingering yourself. Watch some porn."

Clearly, this was important to her, and since I'm what sex columnist Dan Savage coined as "good, giving, and game"—or GGG—I decided I'd stick my fingers in my asshole.

Back at my apartment, I grabbed my laptop, queued a few nasty videos, and placed it on the sink across from the shower. Then I hopped into the hot shower. Very foolishly, I didn't use lube. For reasons unclear, I insisted on squirting conditioner on my finger and slid it in.

It felt . . . weird? Definitely not pleasurable, but also not painful. Being contorted like a pretzel didn't help. Apparently, it's hard to finger your asshole while standing up in the shower.

When I expressed my lackluster experience to Jenny, she again chastised me for doing it wrong. She then asked if she could gently finger me while blowing me. I agreed because I was such an amazing boyfriend.

Now I know the phrase "life-changing" is thrown around often, but I think we can all agree that the banana you had for breakfast wasn't life-changing. However, the first time you stick a banana in your ass? *That* is life-changing.

Jenny was a pro and was quick to find my prostate. Gently, she massaged it, and in the words of America's favorite twink, Troye Sivan, I bloomed. Within minutes of digital penetration, I came my face off. It's tough to describe what it's like to orgasm while having your prostate stimulated, but I'm a writer, and describing things is my job, so I'm going to give it a shot.

For me, orgasming from strictly penile stimulation is like driving a car when you turn sixteen. It's cool and exciting! You're driving a fucking car. You can go places you couldn't go before. You have freedom. Yay! But by the time you're thirty, driving a car isn't as cool as it used to be. Yes, you can have some fun drives on the open road, but it's not as exhilarating as when you were sixteen.

When you orgasm with a finger, vibrating prostate massager, or dick in your rear end, it's like learning your car had wings. You could have been flying this whole time. Do you know what never gets old? A FLYING CAR.

In the end, I think Jenny regretted showing me that my car had wings because suddenly sex was all about my booty. Once Pandora's box was open, there was no closing it. *Oh, my beautiful girlfriend who looks like Charlize Theron wants to get fucked? LOL. I don't see how my butt's involved, so sadly, I will not be able to assist her.*

To this day, if I'm having trouble cumming, I put a little vibrating toy in my bootyhole, and BAM, it's like Old Faithful, erupting right on queue.

While I think it's unexpected that a woman got me to fall in love with anal when countless men beforehand had begged to get into my tender hole, I don't think it was accidental. Her approach was softer. It wasn't a "let me get in that ass" approach that many tops take. She was more delicate, even if firm. She also emphasized *my* pleasure. This wasn't just going to feel good for her; it was going to feel amazing for me. She wanted me to experience the earth-shattering ecstasy from a pinky in the bootyhole for my sake because she loved me and wanted me to experience as much pleasure as possible.

Then, of course, I felt safe with her. She wasn't a stranger at a bar. She wasn't a headless torso on Scruff. She was my girlfriend, and I knew she wouldn't ram it in there and start plowing me. She was going to be gentle, at least at first. As someone who'd gotten fucked on countless occasions in more than one hole, she knew what it was like. She wouldn't be a dick; she would just use her dick.*

I will be forever grateful for Jenny, who encouraged me to explore this new underworld of pleasure. The anus is a magical little hole, and like the door to Narnia, when you open it, you enter a mystical realm full of surprises. And just like with that Narnian door, you're surprised by just how much you can fit inside.

X X X

If asked, I imagine anyone would say they want to have the most pleasurable sex possible. But there is a reason why everyone isn't having incredible sex: It requires communication, vulnerability, and knowing—*owning*—what you like. So when you're having average or slightly above average sex, which can still feel good, it's easier to continue having that type of sex instead of putting in the work to make it superb. It's like how it's easier to make significant changes in your life when things are going poorly, but when things are going "fine," it becomes a lot harder to implement change.

It also takes a ton of courage for a straight, cis man to tell his straight, cis girlfriend, "I want to explore my back door." She might assume this desire means he's secretly gay or bi. She may even leave him at the mere suggestion of it. Yes, that is a real risk. Women can buy into masculine tropes, too; many believe that guys aren't "real men" if they like a pinky (or more) in the booty. Even if they don't think their partner is sexually interested in men, they still might think less of him for wanting to take on a more traditionally submissive sexual activity.

---

*I believe all straight men should have to get fucked in the ass before they fuck a woman. It should be a prerequisite.

Evidently, homophobia affects everyone—even straight, cis couples trying to have good sex. But fun fact: You can be 100 percent straight and like getting pegged, and more straight men enjoy this than you might think. Prostate stimulation has nothing to do with sexual orientation, but it has all to do with powerful orgasms. It is a matter of anatomy—of science!

Frankly, it's ridiculous that, culturally, bottoming somehow implies submission (regardless of sexual orientation). I have topped 250-pound power bottoms, and there is absolutely nothing feminine or submissive about these dudes. They run the show, and at any moment could snap my dick off with their hole. (If they did, worth it!)

When you add racial and ethnic tropes (think: machismo culture), it becomes even more daunting to discuss your sexual desires openly. I'm a little Jewish faggot from Los Angeles. I had it easy, all things considered. Luckily, I have some thoughts on how we can separate anal sex from sexual orientation and make booty play less taboo. Hot load incoming!

Gender is a construct, a social experiment. That's not my hot take. We've all heard this a million times by now. Usually, it's said in the context of attempting to dismantle how restrictive gender norms are. It's an ideology that posits one doesn't have to present their gender in any constrictive way because gender isn't *real*. It's a figment of our imagination. While I agree wholeheartedly, I do not think we, and by "we" I mean the world, will ever rid ourselves of gender stereotypes completely. I'll take it a step further and say that it is not helpful to think of gender as a thing that needs to be abolished. Gender can be a useful framework for folks to feel validated (trans folks included) through the shorthand it provides.*

---

*It's also fun to play with gender. I think we often forget this because of the constant attacks on trans and nonbinary people. Of course, we don't want to trivialize the experiences of trans/nonbinary folks—but it can, simply put, be fun to wear lipstick, a miniskirt, and heels when you identify as a cis man.

Of course, gender expectations and norms can lead to transphobia, misogyny, homophobia, and a ton of other bad shit. However, gender in and of itself is neutral. It's just a form of expression or a lens through which we view the world. I think what we need to do is expand our definition of what it means to be a man and what is included when we discuss the monolith that is "masculinity."*

Recently, many Western cultures have made progress accepting nonbinary and trans folks (with some obvious major setbacks). I've noticed that this acceptance often comes from a reinforcement of gender, which I find worrisome. You should be able to be a man who wears dresses and lipstick and still be a man. Clothing is genderless. Makeup is genderless. So, too, is painting one's nails. While you can (and should) absolutely identify as nonbinary if the identity speaks to you, you can also be an "effeminate" man and still be just that, a man—and a straight man at that! Everything that falls outside the *super* narrow confines of "masculinity" isn't automatically queer.

I think if we allowed men to be more "effeminate" without quickly labeling them as queer, we'd have significantly less homophobia/queerphobia. This means queers need to stop assuming that if a guy likes anal, he must be secretly gay. Oh, you thought I forgot about you? Queers contribute to the problem, too! We are the QUICKEST to assume men are queer if they do *anything* remotely outside the masc, straight box. I know this isn't coming from a malicious place. We just want everyone to express themselves openly. You also want him to dick you down. However, when we label straight men as gay because of their interests (e.g., loving pop divas), their knowledge (e.g., knowing too much about Laura Dern's career), or their actions (e.g., experimenting with another guy), we contribute to the problem.

---

*We also need to expand "femininity" so that women feel more confident taking more active sex roles and dicking down their men.

There's a reason the phrase "no homo" made its way into our vernacular—outside of very blatant homophobia. Straight men felt the need to distance themselves from anything that could be considered "gay" because they were teased, bullied, and harassed for something as innocuous as hugging another male friend.* Since straight men wanted to be able to hug their friends without being ridiculed, they started saying "no homo" after doing *anything* that they thought made them less of a man. "No homo" probably wouldn't have become as pervasive a saying if straight men were allowed to act in manners that are traditionally thought of as being more feminine.

Fearing judgment for expressing platonic intimacy with another man is also a long-standing result of homosexuality being illegal in some parts of the world up until very recently. It still is in others. And even in places where it's legal, like the United States, there are plenty of people and governmental bodies in power that would have it otherwise.

I hope I'm not sounding like a straight man apologist. No man—or any person—should be homophobic. No one should belittle, ridicule, and/or assault queers, and there's no excuse for that behavior. However, I think it's clear that preaching tolerance and acceptance isn't enough. We need to acknowledge that homophobia is learned and that these people are products of their environments. We need a paradigm shift.

We live in a world where homophobic acts reinforce masculinity and straightness. How fucked-up is that? How did we reach a point where harassing a little gay boy in a crop top makes you more of a man? Why is it still considered "masculine" for high school jocks to call each other "faggot"? This all speaks to why we should not judge men for acting in ways that are perceived as gay or effeminate. We need to expand our notions of masculinity and straightness to arrive at a place where straight men can participate in femininity, too, without someone

---

*Fellas, is it gay to crave human connection?

crying gay wolf. Because guess what? Those men *are* straight. You can crave getting railed by your trans girlfriend's dick or your gf's twelve-inch dildo. You're still straight (and also impressive).

Now if after a few times of experiencing toe-curling pleasure with your girlfriend, you realize that you *also* crave the touch of a man—you want to lick some hairy pecs—you should probably slide into my DMs. You know, for science.

CHAPTER 11

A PEG FOR EVERY HOLE

(Mom and Dad, for the love of God, skip this chapter!)

The fastest I ever came was when I was fourteen. By then, I had moved from nudie mags to internet porn. At first, I had vowed to steer clear of the harder stuff, but there was no escaping it. Every X-rated site's home page was flooded with rough gangbangs, fisting, water sports, rape roleplay, incest, and, appropriately, cum. Even the one-on-one vids were aggressive. I remember typing in "missionary sex" hoping to see something tamer. While, yes, the performers had sex in the classic position, the man still choked, slapped, and spit on the woman. The porn industry clearly didn't understand the underlying vanilla tone of someone searching for missionary sex videos.

It wasn't long before I found a very intense blow job scene. The woman was lying on her back with her head over the edge of the bed; a very well-endowed man was aggressively deepthroating her. I could see her throat protrude with the outline of his penis each time he thrusted. I had never seen anything like it before and was shocked that the human body was physically capable of expanding this way. I was even more shocked by how quickly I came. Why did *that* do it for me?

During my next session, I tried to find similar videos, but this was during the earlier days of the internet, and I had no idea how to properly search for content online. I didn't even know the terms "throatfucking," "skullfucking," or "facefucking." (Such aggressive terms!) All I knew was deepthroating, which almost delivered the content I was seeking, but not quite.

Eventually, I stumbled on the correct words: "throat bulge" or "deepthroat bulge." Bulge porn led me down a rabbit hole where I watched very "messy" blow jobs with spit absolutely everywhere. This eventually progressed to an even more extreme version of messy throat-fucking: deepthroat puking. I simply could not get enough throw-up videos, and that urge never subsided. I still love it to this day, in porn and real life. It doesn't matter whether someone's puking on my dick or I'm puking on theirs; I'm an equal opportunist vomit fetishist! The term for this is emetophilia. While emetophilia broadly means arousal from vomit, I fall somewhere in a subsection where a penis has to be involved; I'm not turned on by puking because someone's ill.

My puke fetish has led to very rewarding and very embarrassing experiences. I was once on a date with a media personality who's self-proclaimed life mission was to destigmatize sexual shame among gay men. We got drinks and started making out in the bar. I suggested taking it back to my place, where I learned his dick was comically large. It was like his dick ate two of my dicks, and I just knew I had to puke on it. I asked if he would be into it; he said he was, so I put a towel underneath him and went to town.

The next day I sent a generic text: "Had a ton of fun with you and would love to see you again sometime." No response. I sent a follow-up a few days later: "What's your schedule like this week? I would love to take you out!" Again, no response. Considering before I put a towel down, the night went super well—we had a long, vulnerable heart-to-heart where we shared so much about our romantic lives—I have to believe my kink scared him off.

Fair enough. Sometimes revealing fetishes on a first date can feel a little aggressive to folks. However, since we spoke in *detail* about various ways gay men have kinky sex, I thought we could get weird. I also asked him if he'd be into it, and he said yes; I don't go around throwing up on dicks without warning!

Jordan, my current boyfriend or most recent ex, depending on when this book publishes, likes to remind me that I encouraged us getting weird on our second date. After a night of drinking, we went into my office. I placed a towel down on my office chair and then went to town. (Again, I asked if he would be into it, and he said, "Sure!") He wasn't clear how aggressive he could be and was erring on the side of caution, as one should. Then I said, "Push my head down hard. Don't let me come up to breathe even if I try."

Well, we're still dating (or not) over two years later, so he didn't hate it. We've since discussed my kink in detail, and I learned he initially felt indifferent. Considering it was such a massive turn-on for me, he was more than happy to oblige. He also appreciated it as a new sexual experience.*

There's something to this—I'm not just recounting my favorite vomit tales to gross you out (or turn you on). You don't always need to find a sexual partner who's incredibly aroused by your kink; you simply need someone who's open to trying new things and enjoys pleasing their partner. I've had a kink partner for over five years who absolutely loves it when I piss in his mouth. It does nothing for me, but I'm also not turned off by it. Seeing the amount of pleasure he gets from it *does* turn me on immensely. So after we have some rough sex, I piss in his mouth. He loves it, and I don't get a UTI.

Up until recently, I didn't share my puke kink publicly. I didn't write about it or tell my friends when we talked about what we're into. As you may have figured out by now, this is pretty atypical for me. I am a Millennial who's made a career of oversharing my sexual exploits, but something about this kink left me shameful. I'm fully aware that it's a more intense kink. I also feared being judged, worried people would

---

*I should note that I also have non-kinky sex—in fact, most of my sex isn't kinky—and I watch plenty of other non-kinky porn.

think I was mentally ill, and fretted that my sexual inclinations would somehow invalidate my work as a sex writer. I imagined the Fox News takedown piece: "*Men's Health* Sex Columnist Encourages Bulimia . . . with His Penis."

But in September 2019, I received an unexpected call from an acquaintance, a professional dominatrix, sex educator, and co-creator of an event called Pass the Porn, where folks gathered at House of Yes to watch pornos of a specific kink, and then sex educators spoke about that kink on a panel. She asked me if I wanted to be a speaker on the "food play"* panel.

I had previously told her in confidence about my puke fetish, and she thought it would be an illuminating addition to the topic. I wasn't sure if my fetish really fell under the sploshing umbrella, and while she agreed that it was adjacent, she thought people would enjoy learning more about emetophilia. Since I wasn't sure if I was ready to disclose my kink to the world, I told her I'd have to think on it.

But the more I thought about it, the more uncertain I became. I was entitled to privacy—I had already shared so much in my work—but I ultimately agreed because not wanting to share was based in fear of rejection and shame. I needed a dose of my own medicine. How could I encourage people to embrace their kinks and desires without following suit?

Still, I didn't widely publicize the event. On the day of the panel, I had nonstop diarrhea, which was how I knew I was nervous. (My gut is always the first to let me know when I'm anxious.) Even though I knew folks in that space wouldn't shame me for my kink, I still worried my kink was more intense than theirs. *Oh, you like feeding your partner strawberries during sex and having them lick whipped cream off your titties? Cool! I like it when I facefuck someone so hard that they puke all over my dick.*

---

*Often referred to as sploshing.

I came early, something I do when I'm nervous and/or aroused. I mingled until the porn began—a few artsy videos that involved food play. Some of them felt like short films worthy of debuting at Sundance. Then it was the panelists' time to shine. Onstage, sandwiched between the other speakers, I couldn't make out the large audience because the lights were blinding. After the moderator briefly introduced us, she asked us to share our own personal relationship with food, sex, and porn.

I did not volunteer to go first, but eventually my time did come, and I had to explain: "So I'm less interested in food going into the mouth than food coming out of it." I paused, hoping that would be enough, but realized that my intentional vagueness was too vague. "I like it when people puke on my dick."

"Oh, very interesting," the moderator replied. While she knew this was my kink and why I was there to speak, she still acted appropriately surprised. "Is there any type of puke you prefer? Do you have them drink or eat something prior?"

It wasn't a question I had thought much about. Up until this point, my puke fetish was more opportunistic rather than a planned scene. A guy on Grindr says, "I love being throatfucked super hard." I ask if he likes it so hard that he pukes. If he says "Fuck yes," then I reply, "Get that sloppy mouth over here." Fifteen minutes later, I put down a towel and the festivities begin. I'm not exactly at Trader Joe's, strolling the frozen food section, wondering what will look or feel best coming back up, though the answer is obviously their chicken tikka masala.

"Well," I began, "once a guy who had just eaten an entire hamburger an hour earlier puked that up, and it was disgusting." The audience laughed with me. "It wasn't an issue of the texture, though I've learned I'm not a fan of chunky puke. It just smelled really gross."

"How about any liquids?"

"Milk!" I replied. "I first saw it in porn and got turned on, so I tried it out. And when milk comes back up, it doesn't smell nasty. The white is also aesthetically pleasing."*

"So aesthetics also come into play?" she asked. Frankly, I wanted her to stop because I didn't know how to answer her questions. This was unlike me. Before every interview or panel, I think of the questions I'm most likely to be asked and prepare responses, but I didn't this time. I was so nervous, I forgot.

"I guess so," I eventually said. "But it's definitely secondary."

"So what is it that you find arousing about vomit play?" she asked with the same firm sincerity of Oprah in the Harry-Meghan interview.

Another realization: I had never taken time to analyze my own arousal with my kink. While journaling, something I do occasionally, I had never asked myself *why* I like it when people puke on my dick. Is it because I didn't have enough love growing up? Or maybe I was too loved? Is it an oral fixation? I never pondered it; I just, in the words of Sheryl Sandberg, leaned in.

"I actually haven't thought about my kink in this much detail before," I eventually admitted before landing on the idea of purging. "I feel like there's this cathartic release when you puke. You always feel better after you do it and get whatever toxins out of your body. It also differs from typical sex, which tends to involve putting things in instead of things coming out. You stick your dick in a hole. You put your dick in a mouth. Puking is the opposite. It's release."

I was satisfied, rather smugly, with that answer at the time, but as I write it down now, I realize it might not be that deep. While it's a fascinating self-psychoanalysis, I may just be into it for no particular reason, or for the more obvious one: dominance and submission. When

*I learned this from watching Kate Truu, one of my favorite porn stars in the world. I highly recommend you watch her content if you're into messy head.

subbing (i.e., the one puking on the cock), I get a much-needed escape from my anxiety and cyclical patterns of thought. When I'm naked on all fours, gagging on some dick, I'm not thinking about my deadlines. I'm not dwelling on my argument with another partner earlier that day. I'm not obsessing over the hurtful things people say to me on the internet. All I'm thinking is: *Oh shit, I can't breathe.*

The best part is I don't immediately return to anxious spiraling after the scene is complete. I have a couple of days where I feel "Zen." While smoking weed and watching cartoons do provide temporary solace, the moment *Big Mouth* finishes, I'm back to my old, anxious self.

As for when I dom, I like feeling in control. I feel powerful when someone listens to my words and performs extreme acts with their bodies just because I commanded. I could probably analyze this further but frankly, feel no need. More often than not, I don't think there's any value in investigating one's kinks—trying to get at the "root" of a particular paraphilia. I actually think feeling compelled to psychoanalyze comes from a place of sex-negativity. Often, folks feel the need to explain or justify their kinks and sexual desires through past experiences. You don't have to do that. If you're having consensual fun, just enjoy it.*

When Pass the Porn finished, I felt an overwhelming sense of relief. I had shared my most private kink—and to applause! They appreciated my honesty and vulnerability. While many likely did not share my kink, they still knew what it felt like to feel shame around their "unusual" desires. They also saw how therapeutic it can be to share these desires and learned there's a decent chance they won't be

---

*That said, if you're someone who's simply interested in learning about the root of your desires because you find it fascinating—and you're not approaching your introspection with a sex-negative lens—then go for it. However, take all your thoughts with a grain of salt. What we think is the root of a kink might not actually be.

judged (as long as they're surrounding themselves with sex-positive folks). Hell, they may even be asked to speak publicly about them. They may be embraced for something they previously thought of as "off-putting" or "perverted." If they're not fully embraced, at least they'll learn it's not that big of a deal. People really don't care as much about your kinks as you think. They're all too busy worrying about what people think of *their* kinks.

And to my surprise, as I was waiting for my Lyft, a long-haired fellow came up to me and said, "Thank you for sharing. I fucking love it when my girlfriend pukes on my dick, too. That shit's hot."

X X X

As the saying goes, "We all have our kinks." (At least, I think that's a saying. If not, I'm saying it now.) While mine involves a penis in a throat, yours may involve dressing up as a vampire and drinking your partner's period blood. Whatever floats your boat. (That is *definitely* a saying.) As the vast majority of sex educators and therapists agree, anything's okay between two consenting adults.

I've echoed this sentiment, and 99 percent of the time I think it's true. However, I think there are some questionable, arguably problematic kinks worth discussing. For example—and porn has certainly contributed to the prevalence of this one—I don't support a sixty-year-old stepdad sleeping with his eighteen-year-old daughter if he raised her. Yes, we all love a "Daddy," but your stepfather is different. This man raised you, fed you, and wiped your ass—I think this inherent power dynamic precludes the ability to authentically consent.

Neither can I get behind bug chasers. If you aren't familiar with the term, it refers to gay/bi men who specifically seek out HIV-positive guys with a detectable viral load so that they can acquire the virus. I know from my friends living with HIV that bug chasers are not a small subsection of the gay community. All of my poz friends, on multiple occasions, have been asked to "share their gift" on hookup apps.

One friend typically replies: "I'm not going off my medications, putting my life at risk, in order to have a detectable viral load so that you can get HIV." I like this response because it highlights the act's selfishness. You aren't just putting your life at risk, you're putting the other person's life in danger, too.

But as for the other 99 percent of sexual activities occurring between consenting adults? You gotta live and let live. What someone else does in their bedroom (living room, kitchen, or attic . . .) does not concern you. Instead of sticking your nose in other people's business, stick that nose in your partner's bussy. It's 2023, and we (should) know better than to pathologize kinks involving danger, harm, humiliation, degradation, sadism, masochism, and pain.

This wasn't always the case. When I co-authored *Men's Health Best. Sex. Ever: 200 Frank, Funny & Friendly Answers About Getting It On*, I had the pleasure of speaking to Justin Lehmiller, PhD. Lehmiller, a research fellow at the Kinsey Institute, is one of the most prominent kink and fetish researchers in the world. I asked him why there's such a stigma toward kinks and fetishes. Here was his response:

> One reason is that our ideas about sex and sexual morality have a long religious history behind them. In many of the dominant religions, the definition of what is "normal" and moral when it comes to sex is very limited and often refers only to penile-vaginal intercourse in the context of a heterosexual, monogamous marriage and procreation. Since we're taught this from a young age, it's very easy to feel shame, or weird, or that something is wrong with us for having, really, *any* turn-on.

But another part of this has to do with how the mental health community has treated sexual interests throughout history. Historically, sadomasochism was considered to be a deviant sexual interest. Doctors thought that only somebody who has something really wrong with them would be turned on by BDSM. In fact, it wasn't that long ago that sadism and masochism were listed as disorders in the *DSM* [*Diagnostic and Statistical Manual of Mental Disorders*], which is the psychiatry bible. It's only been in the last decade that medical professionals have changed how they talk about kinks.

So now in the *DSM-5*, they have "Sexual Sadism Disorder" and "Sexual Masochism Disorder," rather than just "Sadism" and "Masochism." This updated terminology only refers to cases where somebody's sexual interest is causing distress and problems in their life because it's non-consensual or creating some other type of problem. Increasingly, psychologists and psychiatrists make a distinction between having an unusual sexual interest and having a sexual disorder. That's been a really important shift in the field, but I don't think that the public is even aware of these changes.

Essentially, Lehmiller suggests that BDSM and kinks are problems only when they cause problems. So when they don't, go ahead and touch that lil' dangly thing that swings in the back of my throat.

Nevertheless, I've noticed that a lot of people who struggle with mental illnesses and trauma are drawn to kink. (Not all, but a lot.) This may seem oppositional to Lehmiller's quote, but it's not. Just refer back to how subbing is a way for me to healthily cope with my anxiety.

While I can't speak to how BDSM can be therapeutic to survivors of sexual assault and abuse, a 2021 study published in the journal *Sexual and Relationship Therapy* explored just that. The researchers categorized six "themes" or ways BDSM can be a therapeutic tool to cope with past sexual trauma: "Cultural context of healing (e.g. using BDSM norms and previous therapy to reframe kink and trauma), restructuring the self-concept (e.g. strengthening internal characteristics which had been harmed or distorted), liberation through relationship (e.g. learning to be valued by intimate others), reclaiming power (e.g. setting and maintaining personal boundaries), repurposing behaviors (e.g. engaging in aspects of prolonged exposure), and redefining pain (e.g. transcending painful memories through masochism)."

Participants only reported re-traumatizing themselves when they engaged in BDSM improperly. So when you feel pressured or don't have a safe word, it will likely be a traumatic experience. But if you conduct BDSM with communication and boundaries, it can be a therapeutic experience that helps one overcome past sexual trauma. So yes, health insurers should cover the entrée fee to all kinky, sex clubs.

X X X

If getting onstage to publicly discuss my vomit fetish wasn't reassuring enough, the work I do elsewhere has certainly made me feel less alone in the kinky wilderness. I cannot tell you the number of kink-related questions I receive for Sexplain It. While each person's situation and kinks vary, they tend to share a common factor, seeking an answer to the same underlying, existential (and flawed) question: Am I normal? *Is it normal that I want to be breastfed and jerked off at the same time? Is it normal that I can only get hard while having my ass eaten? Is it normal that I want to be called a "pathetic loser" while getting railed?*

I can't answer these questions because there is no such thing as "normal" when it comes to sexual desire. Everyone is different. But I can say that it doesn't matter whether your sexual desires are "normal" or not. Let's say you're sexually aroused by dirt. This specific paraphilia is called mysophilia. Why does it matter if you want to fuck outside on a dusty trail? The only thing that matters is being able to find others who are into some dirt(y) play, too.

Don't get me wrong. I understand the natural desire to fit in, to like what everyone else likes, and to do what everyone else does. Being different is hard. We all know this, especially queer people. It's scary and often lonely, but living your life doing what everyone else does won't bring you joy. That's what separates people from sheep.

I get it, though—you still might not be able to shake this idea that you are perverted. Your particular kink is *so* fucked-up even though all parties enthusiastically consent. First off, I didn't come down *that* hard on bug chasers, so put your kink into perspective. Second, while I can't speak to kinks being "normal," I can speak to their prevalence.

Well, I can speak to how common it is to *fantasize* about kinks. Alas, there isn't much data on the prevalence of mysophilia and emetophilia. It turns out the NIH isn't opening its pockets to researchers asking hard-hitting questions like, "If we collected all the piss from those engaging in water sports, how many pools would it fill?"

For his book *Tell Me What You Want*, Lehmiller surveyed 4,175 Americans aged 18–87 about their sexual fantasies and found out exactly which kinks people daydream about the most.

BDSM was the most popular. Ninety-three percent of men and ninety-six percent of women had fantasized about some aspect of BDSM before. Of course, BDSM reflects a wide spectrum, from light spanking to vomiting on someone's penis, but it speaks to the fact that most people are not *just* vanilla in bed. Or at least they're not thinking vanilla thoughts. Just because you fantasize about some sexual behaviors doesn't mean you want to act on them, and some fantasies (i.e., non-consensual fantasies) should never be acted upon. Still, I'd wager many people are acting on their fantasies, or they would act on them if they didn't feel any shame.

Kinks are common. Fantasizing about kinks is common. Acting out kinks is common. If you're defining "normal" by "are other people doing this shit?" then yes, you're normal, because other people are doing kinky shit, too, sometimes involving actual shit.*

I believe there is power in sharing our kinks, in "normalizing" them. (I mean, there better be. Otherwise I would have kept my vomit fetish private.) Once we acknowledge how common kinks are, whether or not someone shares your exact kink, we begin the self-acceptance process. This allows us to start talking openly about our desires with our partners, which leads to happier, healthier, and more satisfying relationships.

And remember, even if only .01 percent of the population has your kink, roughly eight hundred thousand people are into the same weird stuff you are. And there are bountiful ways to meet them—get on Recon, FetLife, #open, Scruff, KinkD, Grindr, Whiplr, Feeld, Sniffies, or any other app or site catered to kinky folks. Thanks to this new cool invention called the internet, it has never been easier to connect with people who share your kinks. You can do so anonymously from your home. Then when you find someone else who also likes to dress up as a baby and have sex, you two can meet up and *goo-goo ga-ga* together.

You could also hire a sex worker. Sex workers are professionals who will not shame you. They are experts at creating an environment where you feel safe to explore sexually; that's literally their job. And if you're worried about being nervous with a sex worker—and you wouldn't be alone here—remember that sex workers know how to handle nerves and shame. I could not think of a more ideal situation for exploring a kink.

---

*By this definition, vanilla sex is actually abnormal because you're in a minority if you're not fantasizing or acting out something kinky. This makes being vanilla one of the kinkiest kinks of them all! So if someone ever tries to vanilla-shame you, just tell them you're not a basic bitch who's into BDSM like everyone else.

If you're thinking, "Wow, Zach, you're so hot, you've definitely never hired a sex worker!" I say, thank you for thinking I'm hot. However, being hot has nothing to do with hiring a sex worker, which is why you're dead wrong! For one, I have done sex work. I love money, and I love sex, so it's a great fit for me. Two, I hire sex workers but for different reasons—sometimes I want to have sex with someone new and not have to go through the rigmarole of Grindr; sometimes I want to have sex, and then immediately afterward kick them out without feeling like an asshole. Then there are sexy himbos and self-proclaimed bimbos on Twitter I follow who are sex workers, and I want to have sex with them, specifically. Since their job is sex work, they're not in the business of handing out free fucks, so I happily pay.

Whether you go the route of hiring a sex worker, chatting/meeting with kinksters online, or sliding into my DMs, you gotta start opening up about your kinks to *someone*. It's okay if the first person you choose isn't open to your kink—that's not an indictment of you, it just means they're not into it. To each their own. But if you continue to seek out those who share in your desires, you'll eventually find a good fit. It's hard work putting yourself out there, but the rewards are plentiful. I mean, who doesn't want to have shameless sex? (Unless, of course, shame is your kink.)

But before you start discussing and exploring your kinks, I want to impart one last pearl (necklace) of wisdom. In my experience, when you are ashamed of something, others will shame you. When you're embarrassed by something, others will pity you. If you present something as problematic or deviant, you will be treated as a troubled freak. That's why you need to own your kinks. When you talk about how you like being led on a leash and called a "good boy," say it the same way you would tell a server, "I'd like an omelet with feta, asparagus, and shrimp." Both are things you like. It's that simple. You don't preface a server with "I know that's a bizarre combo of things to put in an omelet, but . . ." You just say what you fucking want.

I overcame this hurdle and wholly owned my sexuality when I spoke about my kinks in front of a live audience. I'm not saying or recommending that you do the same. Well, I don't *not* recommend that for you either, but don't forget I had daylong, nerve-induced diarrhea. Still, literally being in the spotlight and owning my pleasures helped me to arrive at a place of embrace and to move away from one of hesitation, embarrassment, and shame. And I've got to admit, it feels really fucking good.

Nevertheless, baby steps. Start by opening up about your fetishes in a safe, kink-friendly environment. Once you feel a little less insecure about them, tell a few close friends. Then tell your partners. Then, finally, get weird and enjoy it. And if you're into emetophilia, come find me at a book signing.

CHAPTER 12

FOOL ME THREE TIMES

When I heard my number called over the loud-speakers, I stood up, readjusted my crotch, and headed back into one of the treatment rooms. By then I knew the drill. I was a regular at the New York City Department of Mental Health and Hygiene (aka *the* clinic). Like clockwork, I'd come in every three months, if not sooner. This time, it happened to be sooner.

When Nancy (the nurse practitioner's name is always Nancy) asked, "What brings you in today?" I replied, "I have gonorrhea."

"How are you sure?" she asked. "Did a partner tell you that they tested positive for gonorrhea?"

Without saying anything, I dropped my neon-yellow briefs and squeezed my penis, emitting a goo the same color as my undies.*

"Yep. That definitely looks like gonorrhea to me," Nancy said.

She gave me the usual: a shot of 250 milligrams of ceftriaxone in my left butt cheek, 1,000 milligrams of azithromycin, and a recommended seven-day hiatus from all sexual activity.†

This would be my third time in eighteen months I had tangoed with gon-gon (sounds less scary with a cute nickname). When you're someone like me who's had unprotected sex with hundreds of women,

---

*Yes, I had purposefully worn a pair of underwear that matched my discharge. It's called *fashion*.

†FYI, in 2020 the CDC changed treatment. It's now a 500 milligram intramuscular dose to treat uncomplicated gonorrhea. If Chlamydia hasn't been ruled out, like in my case, the CDC recommends taking seven days of doxycycline instead of one dose of azithromycin.

men, and nonbinary babes, the first time you get it, you think, *Well, this was bound to happen. Honestly, I'm surprised it hasn't happened sooner.* The second time you think, *All right, this wasn't a one-time thing. Maybe I should consider changing my behavior.* But fool me three times? That's when you, a sane person who learns from their mistakes, would likely think, *I need to get my act together.*

Like any good Nancy should, Nancy gently but firmly chimed in as I pulled up my pants, "From your record, I see this is the third time you've tested positive for an STI. So you're going to start wearing condoms now, right?"

I paused a second before flashing her a big smile. "No," I replied. While she stood there paralyzed, I gave her a hearty "Thank you very much." Fool me three times, my ass!

Getting gonorrhea sucks. I'm not going to pretend it's on my agenda between bottomless brunch and drunkenly trying on clothes I can't afford in SoHo. It's painful, and in my case, you go through a pair of underwear every two hours. Not to mention you then have to tell all the partners you've had sex with. Responses vary. The guy I met on Grindr who left his apartment door ajar for me to come in and "feed him my load" was, predictably, chill. He simply thanked me for telling him and said he'd get tested and treated that week. It wasn't his first rodeo.

One guy I liked wouldn't see me after I told him. Either my diagnosis frightened him or he started to view me differently. I texted him to check in to see how he was feeling a few days after revealing my positive diagnosis. He gave a monosyllabic "Fine." When I asked if I could take him to dinner to make up for the trouble, he didn't reply.

Still, that's a relatively tame response. I've had some people freak out. I even had one straight woman call me the f-word when I told her she'd been exposed to gonorrhea. (Faggot, not friendzies.)

So, why don't I start wearing condoms? That seems like a logical question.

For one, it can be really hard for me to orgasm wearing condoms. Yes, I'm aware I sound like *that* dude. But for the record, I always wear a condom if my partner wants me to, no questions asked. I never make my inability to cum with a plastic bag on my dick their problem. Because that would be manipulation. And manipulating people is fucking ~~gay~~. (My editor just informed me I am not allowed to "bring back" gay as a pejorative. In fact, he said, that's very ~~gay~~ uncool.)

Remember, I'm a sex writer by trade. I've used all the tricks in the book to help remedy the situation. I've masturbated wearing those thick condoms they hand out at clinics. I've put lube inside the condom and on it. I've used silicone lube as opposed to water-based. I've also abstained from masturbation for days in preparation for a sexual encounter. I figured the buildup would help.

And these things have helped! I *have* orgasmed inside a condom hundreds of times. Also, my partner and I can always just take the condom off when I'm ready to cum and do some hand and mouth stuff to get me there. I LOVE hand and mouth stuff. So sex is still enjoyable with a condom, but yeah, I definitely prefer not to use one when my partner(s) doesn't want me to. I mean, have you had condomless sex? Simply divine.

Second, and what most people—even healthcare professionals—don't understand is how bareback sex impacts my queer identity. I grew up with a healthy fear of STIs, particularly HIV. My middle and high school health classes scared the living shit out of me. In eighth grade, I had a teacher like Coach Carr from *Mean Girls*. Only "Don't have sex because you will get pregnant and die" became "Don't have sex because you will get AIDS and die." Or at least that's how I interpreted what she said. Who the fuck knows? I was an OCD-ridden mess.

When I started having unprotected sex with my girlfriend, who, like me, was a virgin until we began having sex, I would get tested for

HIV for no goddamn reason. My pediatrician was like, "What the fuck are you doing here? Go home. I have REAL shit to deal with. Didn't you hear? Parents are not vaccinating their kids."

Then I started having sex with men, and that's when my fear of HIV skyrocketed. There was a much more legitimate risk of acquiring the virus. Even while wearing a condom, there was, without fail, a point during sex when I thought about getting HIV. If you want to know the ultimate boner killer, it's imagining an emaciated Matt Bomer in *The Normal Heart* covered in lesions while you're trying to get your rocks off. And Matt Bomer is stupidly hot.

This led me to not fully enjoy having sex with men, which complicated my coming-out process further because I couldn't tell whether it was the sex-with-men part that I didn't like or my fear of contracting HIV.

Then I learned about Truvada, a medication that can be taken as PrEP. A little refresher: Truvada is a once-daily pill that decreases the likelihood of acquiring HIV through sex by over 99 percent and is often referred to as "gay birth control." It was approved in 2004 to treat people living with HIV and was then repurposed and approved as a means of PrEP by the FDA in 2012.

The first time I had unprotected anal sex with a man was in May 2013. I learned about PrEP shortly after but didn't start on it until the end of 2015. Once I began using PrEP, my worries vanished. Well, not immediately. It took some time after being on PrEP to stop worrying. My fear ran too deep. Even though the FDA was like, "Dude, you'll be fine. Chill out and breed that hole." I was still like, "Are you sure? Like, really sure?"

Many straight people take the act of sex for granted. That's completely fine. I'm not trying to shame any straight readers. Go live and fuck. The world is your oyster, and oysters are an aphrodisiac! Besides, I don't blame you for not thinking about HIV or other men when having sex with your wife. If you are, then I think it's very good that you, sir, in particular, are reading my book.*

But having sex is far more complicated for gay and bi men. Many of us, especially when first starting to have sex, feel shame, self-loathing, and confusion. Many queer men get over it, but I still have friends who are out as gay but cannot have sex with another man sober. You'd think they would have faced the realities of their attractions before coming out publicly, but that's not always the case.

Then there's the fear of HIV. Let's say you finally get over the self-hatred and confusion of having sex with other men. You still can't enjoy boning because you're thinking about a virus that could change the course of your life.†

There are few worse feelings than really liking a man, finally getting to the point of having sex, and not being able to because you think about all the gay men who've died from AIDS complications. You think about all the love, art, and overall good these men could have brought to the world. You think about the devastating ends of their lives— how they felt, what they missed, and who missed them after they were gone.

By 1995 in the United States, one in nine gay/bi men had been diagnosed with AIDS and one in fifteen had died; about 10 percent of the 1.6 million men aged 25–44 who identified as gay had died. More than seven hundred thousand people in the United States have died since the virus' inception, predominantly gay/bi men. The World Health Organization estimates that 36.3 million people—gay, bisexual, and otherwise—have died worldwide.

It's not quantifiable, but I'd bet the widespread misinformation,

---

*Also, you totally can get HIV from vaginal sex. HIV doesn't just affect gay/ queer men.

†Luckily, HIV is a manageable virus these days. With modern meds, you can live a healthy and normal life. But of course, this wasn't always the case, and many of the stigmas of an earlier era still linger today when discussing HIV.

paranoia, and fear surrounding AIDS contribute to the hatred and violence against queer folks. Because the moment queer people step outside our apartments, we're subjected to hate and violence. Not every day. Not every time. And some people more than others.

I still fear holding a man's hand in public, and I'm a six-four questionably muscular dude who lives in Brooklyn. I once had a person on the street yell at me and my boyfriend for holding hands. "I hope you get AIDS," she said. In Williamsburg, a man in a red Porsche tried to hit me with his car. After jumping out of the way, I screamed, and he called me a faggot. It was the summer of 2019, and I was wearing tiny pink cutoff jorts.

My hardships are minimal compared to most queer men and women because of where I live and my ability to "pass" as straight (when I so choose). When I'm not dressing up for an event, I typically wear jeans and a black T-shirt. (Although I will say my shorts are exceedingly revealing come summer.) I would dress more openly queer if I wasn't afraid. But when I wear a crop top while walking home from the train late at night, I know someone could say something, follow me, or even attack me. I haven't been beaten up yet, but I also sprinted away when a group of teens came rushing toward me, shouting "faggot!"

My ex Angelo *always* wore crop tops every time we went out. I don't think he owned a single shirt that covered his midriff, and if he did, he would tie it at his sternum to let his tummy breathe. I asked him once if he was afraid. "Yeah, but fuck them!" he said. He knew the risk of how he presented, but he did it anyway. His bravery was contagious, to the point where I actually started to wear more genderbending clothing.

At one point, he did mention that I seemed to attract more negative attention than he did. He thought it was because I presented more masculine while wearing queer clothing. I still had a beard, muscles, and hairy stomach while wearing a crop top and heels. Whereas he, with his face immaculately beat for the gods, looked very feminine. Angelo said that I looked like I'd be a better fight.

I'm not sure how true that is, but I will say more "straight" men tried to fuck him than beat him up. Perhaps Angelo presented so femme that they no longer viewed him as a masculine threat, whereas I tended to look more physically similar to the aggressors, except for my fabulous wardrobe. Maybe that's why I got harassed more when I wore women's clothing, though that's not what matters. It's not a competition. What matters is that I got and continue to get harassed. So does Angelo. So does every queer person who defies gender norms in their presentation.

Nurse Nancy, as much as I love her, doesn't get all this. She doesn't understand how this plays into queer folks' relationship with sex. Behind closed doors, sex is one of the few things that's ours. It's theoretically one of the few acts that hatred and fear can't touch. It's where we can be our gayest, most fabulous and loving selves.

Thanks to modern medicine, we can enjoy sex without the fear of contracting HIV. We can have the same sexual privileges that straight people enjoy. I want to enjoy sex. I want to have the best sex I can. I want this one part of my life to be completely untouched by fear.

When I have sex without a condom, that's exactly how I feel. That's why I go through the rigmarole of getting tested and treated, telling my partners, and shitting my goddamn pants.* For other people, it's not worth it, but for me, it absolutely is. It's one of those calculated slutty risks that I've analyzed, and the decision that I've come to, while controversial, is mine.

---

*I inevitably get severe diarrhea for forty-eight hours following treatment. One time, while viewing *Spider-Man: Far from Home* at the Regal Essex Crossing theater on the Lower East Side, I did not make it to the toilet in time.

X X X

In the BDSM community, there's something called risk-aware consensual kink, or RACK. It's a philosophical view that permits certain risky sexual behaviors as long as all participants are fully aware of the potential dangers. RACK is contingent on information and awareness. It doesn't work if you don't know what the risks are, which speaks to yet another reason why we need to teach accurate sexual health information. (God, I wish Instagram didn't censor my writing and every other post.)

Still, you do your best to mitigate risks. You have a pair of safety shears when you tie up a rope bottom because you don't want them to lose circulation and get permanent nerve damage. You have a safe word when you engage in consensual non-consensual play (i.e., rape roleplay). With breath play (i.e., choking), you have a "safety action" in case your partner is unable to communicate verbally. Even with these precautions, there are obvious risks.

Not only do I believe in RACK ideologically, I think we should take RACK one step further and apply it to all sexual behaviors. There is always some level of risk when having sex, even vanilla sex. Condoms are not 100 percent effective in preventing STIs. It's why many sex professionals, myself included, have shifted from saying "safe sex" to "safer sex," acknowledging that no type of sex is without risks. Also, you can get an STI from oral sex—I've had mouth gon-gon aka oral gonorrhea a half dozen times—but you don't see people putting on a condom to get some head. We knowingly take these STI risks when we have various types of sex.

Then, sex can be painful. I've got my asshole *torn* up. I've wiped to reveal enough blood to pour on Carrie. I once had an ex nick the head of my penis with her canines while blowing me. Ever seen a penis blood geyser? I hope you never have to. And this was all during non-BDSM sex. Anything can happen. You can fall off your bed and break your hip. You can get a UTI. You can accidentally catch a load in your eye, and that shit stings!

And those are just physical risks. The emotional risks are far more painful and last longer. We open ourselves both literally and figuratively when having sex. Nearly all of us have been hurt emotionally after sex. It may be the one aspect of sex we can all relate to, no matter who we sleep with or how we sleep with them. We've felt used. We've felt neglected. We've felt pressured. We've felt dissatisfied. That doesn't mean we stop having sex; we just acknowledge the risks, do our best to mitigate them, and take the plunge anyway.

As a society, we've deemed that these risks are acceptable. Yet the informed risks that I take, specifically not wearing condoms, are seen as unacceptable. To which I say, well, I've done the research and know that antibiotics treat syphilis, gonorrhea, and chlamydia. As for antibiotic-resistant gonorrhea? I'll admit that this is actually quite worrisome. If (or when) we start to see major outbreaks of antibiotic-resistant gonorrhea, I'll start wrapping it up, but until then, I'm going to keep raw-dogging it.

Moving on to viruses—PrEP keeps me safe from contracting HIV, and nearly everyone has herpes (between oral and genital). The stigma is worse than actually contracting it, which is why the CDC discourages people testing for herpes. Their official stance is: "CDC does not recommend herpes testing for people without symptoms. This is because diagnosing genital herpes in someone without symptoms has not shown any change in their sexual behavior (e.g., wearing a condom or not having sex) nor has it stopped the virus from spreading."

Clearly the CDC doesn't view herpes as a severe health risk. Imagine if they recommended we don't get tested for HIV. They don't say that because there *are* serious health ramifications for letting HIV go untreated. That's not the case for herpes. The point is: Everything is risky. Which is why I believe that we all should be allowed to choose which risks we accept and take, with our partner's consent, of course. Our ability to choose is not only what makes us adults; it's also at the root of our sexual freedom.

X X X

In case this book becomes a *New York Times* bestseller, I have to clarify that I'm not advocating for every queer or straight person to start taking anonymous loads. I don't want the CDC to put me on their hit list, and I'm not trying to overburden our fragile medical care system with an additional ten thousand leaky dudes flooding the clinic halls. Besides, Nancy has a life to get to.

But I am advocating for everyone to remove all shame and stigma around STIs. Let's treat them like strep throat, which is another bacterial infection. I'd go as far as to call strep the "poly infection." I've gotten strep more times than I can count because when one person gets strep in the polycule, everyone does. Yet, no one feels stigmatized or "dirty" for getting strep. Personally, I'm a little annoyed when I get it—no one likes a fever—but I don't feel any shame.

Let us not forget that the stigma surrounding STIs is *designed*. It's designed to keep you from having sex. It's designed to make you feel shame for something completely normal and healthy. There's also a pernicious sexist element—women are judged and treated more harshly for having an STI than men are. But the history of STI stigma runs deep in this world, and my hot take? It's due to our old friend syphilis.

The origins of syphilis are unclear. However, we know for sure that there was a large outbreak of syphilis at the end of the fifteenth century in Europe that began when the French invaded Naples.

They then did what humans always do: acted xenophobically, blaming warring and neighboring countries for the disease. The inhabitants of today's Italy, Germany, and the UK named syphilis "the French Disease." The French named it "the Neapolitan Disease." The Russians called it "the Polish Disease," and the Polish called it "the German Disease." The Turks called it "the Christian Disease," and in Northern India, Muslims blamed Hindus for the outbreak, and Hindus blamed Muslims before everyone just blamed Europeans. This is similar to Trump calling COVID-19 "the China Virus" or how AIDS was initially called GRID, or "gay-related immunodeficiency." There is a long, rich discriminatory history of labeling a disease or virus after a group of people—specifically those you're prejudiced toward.

All the same, syphilis was killing people. It's estimated that up to five million people died from syphilis across Europe in its heyday. It also had some gnarly symptoms, including sores, abscesses, ulcers, and severe pain. If you were born with congenital syphilis, you could be born blind or with facial deformities. There was no real treatment or cure until our brilliant friend Alexander Fleming invented penicillin. In the olden days, people attempted mercury injections to treat syphilis. That did not work, and people died. Others tried suffumigation (smoking it out). By now we all know that is not how you cure syphilis, and the process of ingesting fumes is not fun, though to be fair, I've never tried. Knowing me, I could be into it.

So while it's messed up to stigmatize people who contract syphilis, you can at least see a logical origin for the fear. You may end up looking like a leper and die. From there, it's a hop, skip, and a jump to stigmatizing *all* STIs.

Now, however, syphilis is curable—not just treatable. You take that penicillin shot in your juicy ass, ice your butt (not necessary, but personally recommended), and ta-da! All gone! No surprise to anyone, but I've had syphilis. And guess what? It didn't fucking matter! I told my partners. They got treated preemptively, and that was it. I'm still out here spreading cheeks and breeding holes like it's my job—actually, it is my job.

A window of STI destigmatization existed during the sexual revolution of the 1960s–1980s in America. People no longer feared the ramifications of getting STIs (yay, antibiotics), and the free love movement was in full swing. But both the stigma and fear returned with a vengeance because of—you guessed it—AIDS. With AIDS, we saw a massive rise in homophobia and the alleged justification for this hatred. *It's God's way of telling you that being gay is a sin!* Obviously not. Then there were also the racial components of AIDS, since it was labeled an African or Haitian disease. And racism is as American as apple pie.

So, when you shame someone for getting an STI, you're engaging in a *lot* of other shaming that you'd (I hope) likely think you're too wise to fall for: sexism, xenophobia, homophobia, and racism. So, what to do? If you hear from a sex partner that they tested positive for syphilis, or any other STI for that matter, instead of freaking out, simply thank them and see your doctor. If you don't have insurance, the internet can point you to numerous nearby clinics that provide free testing and treatment without requiring insurance.

And remember, you're not alone. According to 2015 data from the CDC, there are roughly 20 million new STI diagnoses in the United States each year. Across the nation, at any given time, there are more than 110 million total (new and existing) infections.

There was also a spike in positive diagnoses since the onset of the COVID-19 pandemic. STIs in the United States initially decreased during the early months of the pandemic in 2020, but then resurged by the end of that year. Ultimately, reported cases of gonorrhea, syphilis, and congenital syphilis surpassed 2019 levels.*

Nothing good comes from freaking out, yelling at, or judging someone for having an STI. Frankly, I think we should celebrate STIs. It means you're getting some, and couldn't we all use a little more action?

FYI, I no longer see Nancy, or rather I no longer see *that* Nancy. Since I'm now on Medicaid, I get tested and treated for free through my primary care physician, a gay man who specializes in sexual health. (It's nice seeing him, because as a gay man living in New York City, he's personally familiar with gay hookup culture. He's aware that the vast majority of men using Grindr and Sniffies in New York City don't wear condoms.)

Just last week, when I headed into his office for treatment because my oral swab came back positive for gonorrhea, there wasn't even a question as to whether I was going to start wearing condoms. Both he and I knew I wouldn't, which was why when he said "I'm supposed to say this because I'm your doctor, but you should start wearing condoms," I just laughed and replied, "Okay, Doc. Sure."

---

*It turns out many of us were taking loads when we claimed we were social distancing.

PART IV

SEXUAL
PRIDE

CHAPTER 13

ONCE A CHEATER, ALWAYS POLYAMOROUS

Part(ner) 1

Apart of me had always wanted to fuck Rebannah. Attached at the hip, Rebecca and Hannah were best friends, and the three of us hung out often since Rebecca drove us to school our senior year.

Rebecca lived with her aunt, Shannon, who thought I was God's gift to the world—or at least God's gift to her niece. Rebecca wasn't the most studious, and Shannon liked that I was decently academic. And like a good Jewish boy, I knew how to schmooze with parents. That's why Shannon wanted me to knock up her niece. This is not hyperbole. Shannon, God bless her soul, was nearly identical to Amy Poehler's character in *Mean Girls*, Mrs. George. She often offered us liquor, always top shelf, which I always drank.

My best guy friends always asked if I would or could fuck Rebannah, and by that I mean either Rebecca or Hannah, and I was always a little too quick to respond, "No, it's not like that."

Obviously I wanted to have sex with them. They were both hot and fun and at seventeen I would have said yes to fucking any woman with a pulse. But Rebannah didn't seem interested in me. This may be because we were indeed "just friends," but it may have been because I was in love and in a monogamous relationship with another girl, Sarah.

I was off the market. Seventeen-year-old Zach would never cheat! I saw infidelity as the utmost act of betrayal and believed only unethical cowards cheated.* And I prided myself on being a mensch. But I'd be lying if I said the thought never crossed my mind, especially as I drove my brother's Prius down to a resort in San Diego to spend a three-day weekend with Rebannah and Shannon.

"It's so much fun," Rebannah said when they initially pitched the weekend getaway. "We get stoned and go to the pool and spa during the day, and then we get drunk and party in the room at night."

"That sounds awesome," I replied. It did sound awesome. That still sounds awesome. "I'm in," I said before thinking through the logistics. Rebannah, Rebecca's younger sister, Vicky, and I would be sharing one room. Where exactly was I sleeping? Was I going to share a bed with them? Was it okay if I slept in my regular underwear, or should I plan to cover myself up more? I had never shared a room with three girls without another boy present. I hadn't slept in the same room with three girls *with* other boys present. But maybe I was overthinking all this. We were "just friends," after all.

While out at the pool, Shannon ordered multiple bottles of Belvedere and mixers for us to drink. Remember, she was the *cool aunt*. Shannon told us to have fun, be safe, and knock next door if we needed anything. She then grabbed Vicky because, at fourteen, she was too young to drink. Or at least, *too* too young.

The three of us did what seventeen-year-olds do when given alcohol: show zero restraint. We took shot after shot like our lives depended on it, which led to Rebannah with their tops off in bed with me on the tiny trundle. It would have made more sense to use one of their queen-size beds, but they, as a unit, came over to me because I—I would *never* cheat.

While I kept saying "No, I can't do this," my rock-hard dick was saying otherwise. So, too, were my lips, which were sucking on

---

*Clearly, I hadn't been in any serious relationships prior. Otherwise, I would have understood the many reasons people cheat that have nothing to do with one's moral compass.

Rebecca's tits in between my feeble objections. And my hands, which, for some reason or another, couldn't seem to stop fingering Hannah.

Shannon walked into our threesome midway through and proceeded to say, "Don't mind me—what happens in San Diego stays in San Diego." In hindsight, I really wish I had fucked Shannon instead.

The next morning my guilt didn't just trickle in. It molly-wopped me across the face. While I enjoyed our hookup—like, *really* enjoyed it—I was now a cheater. I didn't see my infidelity as an isolated act or a drunken mistake; I saw it as something terrible that spoke to who I was at my core.

And, of course, Sarah! I couldn't forget about my girlfriend, the love of my life, the best thing that had ever happened to me. What would she think? She would surely break up with me if I told her, but I had to spill the beans. Otherwise, my guilt would consume me until I shriveled up into a little raisin.

It was only Saturday, and we weren't leaving until Monday evening, but I invented an emergency and left. I started crying the moment I stepped into the car. On the road, I called Sarah. Through my tears I said, "I did something really bad on the trip, and I need to talk to you about it in person. I'm driving back. Are you home? Can I come over?"

"Yeah, come over. Are you safe? Are you okay?"

"I'm safe," I said. "I just did something really bad. I'll tell you in person."

The moment I walked through her doors, I confessed. "I got drunk and hooked up with Rebecca and Hannah." She paused, waiting for me to continue. When I didn't say anything, she replied, "Is that it?"

"Yeah . . ." I replied, waiting for the hammer to fall.

Then Sarah erupted into laughter. "Oh my God, I thought it was something way worse. I thought you killed them or something." My mind could not compute. Murder? That would have been better than what I did. I *cheated*. Had she not heard me?

"Honestly, Zach. I kind of expected it. They're pretty—I know they're your friends—but skanky."

She expected it? She isn't breaking up with me? Did she just call my friends skanky?

"You're not mad?"

"No, not at all."

"Really?"

"Yeah, what you did was just physical. Now, if you loved one of them? That would be a different story. But hooking up? That doesn't bother me."

I couldn't muster a response. I felt like a judge had acquitted me of treason on a technicality.

"I read this Kurt Vonnegut book where the people show their love by rubbing the soles of their feet together. It's like their version of soul bonding. If you did that foot thing with someone else, I would be furious. Does that make sense?"

Sarah was describing the difference between polyamory and an open relationship, well before I was familiar with those terms. Logically, what she said made sense, but I was shocked by how logical she could be about this. I was overcome with emotion, whereas she was levelheaded.

"Yeah, it makes sense," I replied. "But just so you know, I am absolutely not okay with you hooking up with anyone else." FYI, while I do think this one-sided openness is a valid form of non-monogamy, assuming both partners agree, I do think it's selfish and a recipe for disaster. I'm not a fan of imposing rules on your partner, especially ones that you don't follow yourself. I find it controlling. You're also not addressing your insecurities and jealousy. You're avoiding them entirely, and I think they will eventually bubble up, overflow, and end the relationship. (Want to guess what ended my relationship with Sarah?)

She laughed. "I know, Zach. I won't. And for the record, I don't actively want you out there hooking up with other girls, but I understand things happen." I gave her a big hug, and when I pulled away we began making out, which led to the best sex we'd ever had.

A month later, I ended up in a limo with fifteen other girls and three guys for a friend's eighteenth birthday. We all got blitzed on our way to San Diego to see 3OH!3 in concert. If memory serves, Ke$ha opened.

That night, two things happened. First, my drunk ass peed in three red Solo cups in the back of the limo while everyone watched and cheered. Second, I made out with and fingered a buxom girl while everyone, again, watched and cheered.

I told Sarah the next day, and while she did not cheer, she was unbothered. "If you start actually *fucking* these women, please wear a condom."

This time I didn't feel that sense of relief.

"You're not mad at all?" I asked.

She shook her head side to side.

"Not jealous?" I asked.

"Nope."

"Sure, yeah . . . that's great," I mumbled.

About a month later, I broke up with Sarah. It turns out when you have your cake and eat it, too, you end up nauseated, bloated, and regretting your choices. I was more of a wreck about the breakup than she was. I cried so badly that when I got home my mom screamed, "What did she do to you?"

"Nothing, Mom," I shouted back. "I'm just"—I took a deep breath—"sad."

I see the irony: I broke up with Sarah because she didn't get angry when I cheated. I thought her lack of jealousy equated with a lack of love. I believed jealousy meant you cared. It was an uncontrollable display of unadulterated affection.

That's why after Sarah, I liked having girlfriends who got a little jealous. Or let me rephrase that: I liked the fact that they got jealous but didn't like dealing with the manifestations and repercussions of their jealousy. I wanted to flirt with other girls freely, but that would be it. They'd say they were jealous, and I would say, "Aww, you like me," and then nothing in our dynamic would change. But that's not how jealousy works.

With Jenny (aka my anal Sherpa), I was suddenly the one who couldn't control the green-eyed monster. We'd be out, and when a person approached her, I'd involuntarily clench my fists and start eavesdropping from afar. Whenever she brought up her exes, which—in my defense—she did multiple times a day, I'd start to fidget. And her vast sexual experience with kink intimidated me; I was sure she'd eventually leave me for someone kinkier.

She wasn't jealous at all, which made it worse. I judged myself harder because she had seemingly worked through her insecurities whereas I was a juvenile mess.

While I again equated her lack of jealousy with a lack of genuine feelings for me, I also learned just how disgusting and all-consuming jealousy is. It would often strike without warning and spread like a virus through my body. I'd feel jealous everywhere, from my taint to my earlobes.

Nothing ever calmed me. While Jenny repeatedly told me I had nothing to worry about and that I needed to trust her, none of her words ever put my worries to bed. What was worse than jealousy was the shame I felt for feeling jealous. I thought I was better than that. I thought I had a solid grip on my emotions; I wasn't a child who constantly needed reassurance. Apparently, I was.

That's why I never thought I could be in any form of ethically non-monogamous relationship. When people brought up the idea of being "open," I would quickly shake my head and say, "That's not for me." At the time, it wasn't.

Which is why it was strange that roughly a year after Jenny and I broke up, I was living with my boyfriend and his wife.

X X X

When Jenny and I split, I wanted to be a massive slut. I'm talking cum-guzzling, cheek-spreading, spit-in-my-mouth SLUT. I had been monogamous for nearly a year, so back to Grindr I went. The boys flooded into my apartment, and I flooded their holes.

Well, inevitably, one night of steamy hole floodery leads to wanting more. Two guys in particular wanted it again and again. I made it clear that I wasn't looking for monogamy or a boyfriend. Still, both men asked me to be their monogamous boyfriend, and the second man cried when I declined. I felt terrible for hurting him, but if I'm being honest, I was angry. I had been clear. I told them I was getting out of a serious relationship and wasn't looking for anything "committed." They claimed they understood but secretly hoped they could change my mind. When they couldn't, I was the asshole.

After the second "breakup," I decided no more dates—only no-strings-attached sex from there on out. Even a Netflix and chill was too much. Chilling was not on the menu; I wanted them in and out of my apartment within thirty minutes flat, and no, I did not validate parking.

I hit up Grindr harder than ever before, and that is saying something. A new guy every night. And you know what? I was happy! Some people think if you're fucking a new dude every day, you must be unsatisfied. The age-old wisdom goes: While you're filling your bootyhole, the real hole you need to fill is the one in your heart.

But that's what we call sex-negativity!

Sure, some people use sex as a distraction and secretly wish for more intimate connections, but some people just like having sex, plain and simple. They're not unfilled—in fact, they're often quite filled.

Sometimes getting railed feels really damn good. That's it. Let's not overcomplicate things. I had a bunch of casual sex because I liked it. It was a fun activity to enjoy with others. My hobbies included going to museums, working out, watching TV, reading books, and breeding holes.

Then I met Cooper.

We met unexpectedly at Fascination, a monthly leather/fetish party in the basement of Jacque's Cabaret in Boston. That night I was dressed in full garb, serving leather-daddy realness: a leather harness, assless chaps, collar, bracelets, and boots.

I was there with a rich older couple I was boning on the regular when one of them approached me and with light in his eyes said, "Zach! You MUST meet this man we were talking to. He, too, is bisexual!"

Cooper introduced himself with a quiet voice. I could tell he was a little nervous, which I wasn't expecting given his *lewk*. The man exuded Tom of Finland, biker-punk realness. The sides of his head were shaved, with a faux Mohawk on top and braids running down the side. His ears were covered in piercings, and of course a man of his stature had tattoos all over his back. And his ass—oh boy. It was looking really nice in that blue and black singlet. Less to do with his looking like a bona fide badass and more to do with my being obsessed with bubble butts.

After saying hi, he ventured: "You're bi, too." Then there was this painfully awkward pause. What was I going to tell him? "Being bisexual can sometimes be a pain in the ass. Am I right or am I right?" It was weird to be introduced to someone simply because we both had the same sexual orientation.*

He broke the awkward silence by introducing me to his then-boyfriend. Cooper also shared that he had a girlfriend and wife he lived with. My eyes widened. It sounded like a pitch for a mediocre sitcom.

---

*A reminder to well-intentioned mothers everywhere: You don't need to introduce your gay son to every single gay man you meet.

I didn't want to barrage him with the usual questions: "How does that even work?" and "Don't you get jealous?" So instead I asked, "Are you happy?"

He looked at me, perplexed. "What?" he asked. I repeated my question.

He paused, taking time to answer my question honestly. "Yes, I really am," he said.

"Then, do you mind if I interview you?" Even though I wrote about queer relationships, I knew very little about polyamory and thought his relationship dynamic would make for an interesting feature.

Later that week, he invited me over for "family game night." I wasn't sure exactly what that entailed. Would we be playing board games, or was this code for an orgy? Both? Honestly, both sounded ideal. Since I wanted to be prepared for anything, I cleaned out my ass and wore my finest jockstrap under my jeans.

When I entered Cooper's Somerville home, I was quickly introduced to his wife and girlfriend. When I awkwardly waved hello to his wife, Claire, she asked, "Is it okay if we hug? I'm a hugger."

"Of course," I said, and she gave me the warmest hug I'd ever received from a complete stranger. When she finally let go, she was grinning from ear to ear. She was genuinely delighted to meet me—no pretense whatsoever. I couldn't decide if she was like this with everyone or if Cooper had said something about me to her. Whatever the reason, I wasn't complaining.*

I could feel the love bursting in every corner. Everyone hugged. Everyone kissed. Everyone's hand was on everyone else's thigh. Honestly, it was overwhelming, and the more I watched everyone engage with one another, the more I thought their affection felt

---

*I learned much later that she simply is a bubbly, infectiously optimistic, and caring person.

forced. It seemed like everyone was acting overly demonstrative to avoid jealousy or favoritism. It felt like behind all this outward affection, they were hiding something. All the work. The jealousy. The tears. The long talks about making sure everyone's needs were getting met.

By the time I left, I felt foolish to think there may have been an orgy on the menu. More importantly, I was confident that polyamory wasn't right for me. Even though everyone was kind, it all seemed exhausting, so outwardly affectionate and over-the-top.

Still, I liked Cooper. I liked that underneath his badass exterior, there was a shy, compassionate man. Still, I figured there was no future for us—and that was good! I didn't want a boyfriend, let alone a boyfriend who had a wife of eight years and a girlfriend to boot. Nevertheless, I always accepted their invitations to hang out. They were fun, and despite my personal reservations about polyamory, I still found it fascinating. If I'm being completely honest, I felt cool hanging out with poly people. (Back then, I didn't realize that poly people are just a bunch of horny nerds.)

One night, Cooper asked me out on an official first date. I was surprised because Cooper never seemed to have any romantic interest in me, but I agreed because I thought things couldn't get that serious since he already had approximately ten million partners.

Well, one date led to two, and two to a dozen more. Before I knew it, I saw Cooper nearly every day—and I was falling for him. He was smart, hot, and laughed at all my jokes. What more could I want in a man? Two months into dating, we went on a double date with these ridiculously attractive guys we met out at a bar the weekend prior. After dinner, Cooper drove me back to their place for a nightcap, which was thinly veiled code for sex. In the car, drunk, I looked at Cooper. He looked sad, so I asked what was wrong.

"We don't have to do this," I said.

"No, it's not that. I just get worried that you'll leave Boston—leave me," he replied.

I turned to him. "Don't worry. We will figure this out. I love you."

With his smile beaming, he thanked me and said he loved me, too. That was the first time we said the l-word to each other. It was the first time I ever said I love you, romantically, to a man.

"Now you ready to get plowed by two hunks?" I asked.

He laughed. "Let's do it!"

X X X

When Cooper asked me to move in with him and his wife six weeks later, I thought he was kidding. I couldn't help but laugh.

"What's so funny? Why not?" he asked.

"Are you out of your mind? How would this even work?" I asked.

"Never mind. I was just offering," he said.

I didn't mean to hurt his feelings; I was just caught off guard. But in retrospect, it was apparent why he asked me to move in with him after a mere four months of dating. My lease was up, and I was getting ready to move *anywhere* other than Boston.*

I began wondering why I was so quick to reject him. I loved him, we had a great relationship, and I was writing as a freelancer full-time, so I could keep living in Boston, despite it being a pimple on the shoulder of an otherwise great nation.

Did I think our relationship would be one of those "forever" situations? No, and I liked that. I appreciated that polyamorous people don't determine the success of a relationship by how long it lasts. Polyamory doesn't just allow a relationship to evolve; it encourages it,

---

*I found Boston very homonormative and white. Everyone dressed like Young Republican members in their polo shirts and khaki shorts, and the gays there were even more cliquey than usual.

seeing evolution as an inevitability. Sometimes that evolution means growing together, and sometimes it means breaking up and growing independently.

What was I so afraid of?

To be fair, the entire premise sounded unimaginable. Moving in with a man who lives with his wife after four months of dating him? It just sounded ridiculous, for one, and so many things could go wrong, for two. What if his wife got a job somewhere else and they had to move? Where do I go when he has a date at the house? How will I feel hearing him have sex while I'm next door watching TV? What if I feel neglected? What if his wife feels neglected? There was an endless list, each item no more encouraging than the last.

But—BUT—I was in my "yes" phase. I was collecting new experiences like Pokémon. I figured, what the hell—why not take his wife out on an official date and see what it could be like? It wasn't the best reason to ask Claire out, but I wanted one-on-one time with her to discuss some of the reservations about my relationship with him and, well, with her, too.

"It was my idea," she told me during dinner. "I haven't seen him this happy in the eight years we've been married." On the one hand, I was ecstatic that I made Cooper happy, but on the other, what did it mean if he was happier with me after four months than he'd *ever* been with his wife of eight years? That couldn't be a good sign, and how did she feel about that? Was she actually experiencing complete compersion? There was no way she wasn't feeling some type of way—resentment, sadness, anger—*something*. And was it now my responsibility to keep him happy? I knew that wasn't her intent in sharing, but my anxiety was starting to kick in. For fuck's sake, I was about to move in with a married man and his goddamn wife!

"I'm moody," I warned. "I need my own space. I need time to be alone, watch TV, and get a good night's sleep."

"So you're a human being," Claire said. "Good, good, so are we."

"I also can't forgive," I continued. "No three-strike rule. You cross the threshold once, and I'm done with you for good."

"Then we'll have to discuss what your thresholds are, so we don't accidentally cross them," she said.

She was not making this easy—by which I mean she *was* making it easy. She had all the right answers, responding to my every concern perfectly, like a healthy adult. After our conversation, I suggested a long sit-down with all three of us to discuss my needs, concerns, and expectations on the *slight* chance I agreed to share a home with them.

"How does it work if you want to have sex with your date?" I asked once we were all together.

"Since we share our Google Calendar,* you'll know I have a date, so you can leave the house during that time," Cooper replied.

"So it's my responsibility to not be in the house?" I asked.

"No, I mean, usually I'd take the date back to their place," Cooper replied.

"So do we just avoid being in the house when the other person has sex?" I continued.

"No, I mean, you can if you want to. I won't. I don't care," he said. "The first few times you hear it, it's weird, but you get used to it after that."

"Hmm . . ." I said, not at all sold. "This doesn't sound like an ideal situation."

"Honestly, I know it seems like the biggest deal. It's not. You either care, so you leave, or you don't care, or you tell me if it's a problem," Cooper said. "Be vocal."

"FYI, if this doesn't work out, I'm just leaving. You'll find someone to sublet, okay?" I replied, on the cusp of a panic attack. I needed to

---

*There is nothing poly people love more than a shared Google Calendar.

have an exit strategy. I didn't want to be heartbroken living with my ex and his wife. While I hoped that wasn't how things would end, this all sounded too good to be true. Here were these two supportive, receptive, loving people who really wanted me to live with them. Like, *what*? My anxiety was exacerbated by being unable to poke a single hole in their responses; I assumed I'd be able to, but I couldn't. I desperately needed a logical reason for not living there because otherwise, my only reason was fear. And I wasn't going to let my fear stop me from this potentially life-changing experience.

Cooper laughed. "Zach, don't freak out. We'd never force you to live here if you didn't want to."

I was still a nervous wreck after they perfectly addressed my laundry list of concerns, but at least I knew if there was a problem, be vocal. If my needs weren't getting met, be vocal. If I wasn't happy, be vocal. Always be vocal. Communication is key.

So without a logical reason to stop me, I agreed. I was to move in with my boyfriend and his wife. We'd each have our own room. We'd all share a calendar. I'd love him. She'd love him. He'd love both of us. And all three of us would love others.

As they said back then, YOLO.

CHAPTER 14

ONCE A CHEATER, ALWAYS POLYAMOROUS

Part(ner) 2: It's equally as valid and loved as the first part!

I lived with Cooper and Claire for about eight months, and it was one of the best periods of my life. Cooper was my first capital-B Boyfriend. Sure, I had dated guys before—sometimes for months on end—but they never reached Boyfriend status. Having a boyfriend for the first time was fucking awesome. I could do gay things with him. We went to gay bars dressed up like Club Kids. We had a ton of gay orgies. We worked out together. I forced him to watch *Drag Race* even though he didn't like it. You know, gay shit!

But on top of the excitement and generally queer-affirming experience that comes from having a same-sex partner, I loved (living with) Cooper because our relationship was honest in the purest sense of the word. I had a level of transparency with him that I had never experienced before. This wasn't just because polyamory necessitates open communication and expressing your feelings to ensure your relationship(s) don't implode. It was because of how Cooper responded when I would address issues—what therapists like to call "receiving information." He wasn't defensive when I candidly addressed some of his more challenging behaviors.

Cooper struggled with depression. While we'd be out at bars flirting with new people, eventually someone would ask how he was doing, and he'd sometimes say things like "You know, I hate my job, and my life sucks, but I'm not going to kill myself."

"Honey," I'd tell Cooper, "I know you're struggling with your depression, but when you speak so directly about it you really kill the vibe and any chance of us getting laid, making friends, or having a fun time—any way you could keep it lighter when we meet new folks?" He responded with "Shit, yeah, you're right. I'm sorry. I'll try not to do that. It's just hard sometimes to put on a fake smile."

Now most Millennials and Gen-Zers struggle with some form of depression, anxiety, or other mental illness. Most of us have experienced trauma to varying degrees. This may make me sound like a dick, but that doesn't give you carte blanche to do or say anything you want. It also doesn't mean your partner has to support you. Your partner may not have the emotional bandwidth to tend to your needs. It doesn't mean they don't love you. Neither does it mean you're "too much" in general, but it may mean you need to find someone who has a greater emotional capacity to support you. What I mean is: I respected how Cooper owned up to his depression, and it actually allowed me to provide better support.

This was just one of the ways I could be direct and honest with Cooper, knowing he'd be receptive. I felt like I could say anything to him; he'd never get defensive, and I'd never be judged. I let him know if I got bad vibes from one of his new partners, or if I thought one of his friends was taking advantage of him. I wouldn't mince my words when I thought his drug use was teetering on worrisome. And I even told him about my deepthroat puke fetish—he even watched some *nasty* videos with me—and this was way before my panel at House of Yes.

Claire and I did not have a sexual or romantic relationship, which I'd say is more common than a "throuple" or "triad" (i.e., all three people dating one another). Just think how hard it is to find one person you connect with; what are the odds you'd also want to date their partner and all three of you are bisexual and want to date/fuck one another?

Still, I knew I could be as equally up-front with her as I was with Cooper, especially when we were talking about Cooper. Claire and I acted as his parents at times, though not in a condescending manner. Rather, we worked together as a team to figure out the best ways we could support Cooper and each another. This really helped take the edge off when things with Cooper weren't going well. I didn't feel as if I was "alone" in my relationship with Cooper. I had support, and from someone who had been married to him for nearly a decade— a Cooper Whisperer.

It's really frustrating when you don't like or trust your metamours—I've been in those relationships, too. Frankly, that's when drama ensues. But when you have a friendship with your metamour, and you actually like them? That's like finding a straight dude in an Equinox sauna. The relationship doesn't need to be built on a love of your shared partner, though that was the foundation of my relationship with Claire. It can just be that you two like hanging out. "Family game night" isn't just "fun," you feel emotionally sated after a night with your loving, supportive polycule.

This is all to say that Claire and I had an open line of communication and, as far as relationships with metamours go, a pretty solid relationship. Still, this implies that I was seeing and talking to Claire often, which wasn't the case, as she was regularly off canoodling with *her* boyfriend and girlfriend.

While my ability to be direct and truthful about my feelings with Cooper, and for that matter with Claire, didn't actually have to do with polyamory, I owed my ability to step off the relationship escalator and focus on the present to a prominent philosophy in polyamory.

The "relationship escalator" refers to the expected progression of dating to marriage on a standardized timeline. You meet someone. You have sex on the third date. You decide to be monogamous after three months. You say I love you after five. You move in after a year and a half, propose after two years, are married six months later. Then you buy a "starter house" and pump out some rugrats. A few years in, you make some more monies and buy a "finisher house." Finally, you remain married to your spouse until death do you part.

If I sit and think about this for more than a minute, my testicles shoot up into my stomach. This doesn't sound pleasant or comforting to me. It sounds horrifying, like a slow march toward the electric chair. Some people like having their life planned out. I do not. I like the freedom for life to change on a dime—for *me* to change on a dime. I'm not the man I was ten years ago, five years ago, or five months ago; nor do I want to be. To and for me, the escalator feels foolish, an unrealistic restriction on my life(style). I know what works best for me, and so I plan for the future, but I don't plan for forever.

It should come as no surprise that this makes me very ill-equipped to be monogamous. Monogamy's entire apparent success, and even its appeal, is predicated on "forever." Whereas you absolutely can be in a polyamorous relationship forever, and many poly folks want to be, that's not what drives people toward polyamory. It's about the freedom to love many, the potential to grow with and from your partners, the ability to forge your own type of relationship, and the love you receive from your supportive poly(cule) family.*

X X X

My mom—*sorry, Rose*—doesn't miss an opportunity to say that she doesn't think polyamory can ever work. She does, however, think open relationships can. She then points to Cooper, who got divorced from Claire after eleven years of marriage.† When I tell her that doesn't

---

*I mean, also having sex with a bunch of different people.
†This was well after Cooper and I had broken up, and I was in no way responsible for their marriage ending.

mean polyamory failed, they had a beautiful relationship for over a decade, and it's great that they knew when to part ways, she doesn't *really* hear me. She still sees their divorce as evidence that polyamory inevitably fails.

When Cooper and Claire separated, I asked if he thought they would have remained together if they'd stayed monogamous. "Absolutely," Cooper replied. "We would have lived mediocre lives without being fulfilled. We wouldn't have been happy, but we wouldn't have been miserable enough to separate."

Doesn't getting divorced sound a lot better than that?

We like to say "It takes a village to raise a child," but what happens when that child grows up? Why does that village need to disappear? I say, "It takes a village to function as an adult." Not only is it unlikely to find one person who can satisfy all your needs but, oy, the pressure. And do you know what's not good for a healthy relationship? Pressure!

But if I'm going to be blunt—and by now, I think you know I'm going to be—I simply cannot fuck one person for the rest of my life. Is that a joke? Bitch, I am bisexual and need dick and pussy and titties in my face. I need to get railed and spanked but also need to pull someone's hair and choke them out. I need to get called a lil' bitch boy, call him a faggot, and be daddy while also being baby. I need to be in a dark room enjoying a tight bootyhole so much that I don't even notice or *care* when my wallet gets pickpocketed.

I had that sexual freedom even while living with Cooper and Claire. Guys would come over during my lunch break for a quickie. But incidentally, this is what led to our breakup. Not the actual casual sex, but my interpretation of what casual sex meant.

Cooper and I never had great sex one-on-one. I couldn't pinpoint why, since I found him attractive, and he was objectively talented in bed. He wasn't a selfish lover, he communicated, and he was open to trying new things. That's really all you can ask for in a sexual partner.

I convinced myself that I was putting too much sexual energy elsewhere and not focusing on him. It seemingly made sense. When I fucked another guy a few hours before Cooper got home, there was a decent chance I wouldn't have a desire to fuck my main man. So I began to cut out my lunchtime romps, but still, we weren't connecting sexually.

Cooper was perceptive, and one night while we were lying in bed reading, he said, "So it's clear you don't like having sex with me."

His bluntness may seem abrasive, but remember, that's why we worked. We never beat around the bush. Still, I was caught off guard, so I responded, "Why would you say that?"

"Well, do you?"

No, I did not, but I had never said those words aloud. I paused before saying, "I don't."

"It's okay, Zach."

"I don't know why," I continued. "I love you. I find you attractive. You're good at sex, but I get so in my head." *Anddddd* the waterworks began.

"Zach, it's really okay. I know you love me."

"I just can't help but think that something's wrong with our relationship, but I can't figure out what."

"Zach, we don't have to have sex again. We can have a celibate relationship," he said. "It's okay. We both have great sex elsewhere."

"No!" I quickly protested through my tears. "That's not what I want." But looking back on it, that's exactly what I wanted. That would have solved the problem. "If we stop having sex, we're just friends. We're not boyfriends!"

"Whatever you want to do, I'm okay with. I just want you to know that." He really was a great boyfriend.

Alas, this conversation was the beginning of the end. A month later, Cooper asked me if I still wanted to be his boyfriend, and I cried when I told him I did not.

X X X

I thought—hoped—that my inconsistent and infrequent sexual desires ended with Cooper. Moving forward, I would fuck all my romantic partners with the passion of a drunk gay American getting railed on a beach in Mykonos. Unfortunately, my lack of sexual desire became a running theme in my romantic relationships.

For years, I thought something was wrong with me. That I was emotionally stunted or had "commitment issues." That I had an avoidant attachment style. That I was afraid of getting "too close." That I was pulling back before they could hurt me. That I was suppressing unknown sexual trauma. I explored these possibilities and more in therapy, but nothing ever emerged. Besides, I could have intimate relationships with partners. I was open, vulnerable, and loved them dearly. When I took sex out of the equation, my relationships were pretty great.

In 2020, my new therapist informed me of the identity "fraysexual," the opposite of the better-known term "demisexual." Demisexual means you experience sexual attraction only once you've developed an emotional connection with a person. So a demisexual person doesn't see a fine-ass man on the street and think, "Oh shit, I wanna bone."

A fraysexual person experiences sexual attraction toward those they are *not* deeply connected with and loses attraction as they get to know an individual. So, plainly, fraysexuals like to have anonymous and/or casual sex with different folks.*

I cannot tell you how much better I felt when I learned about fraysexuality. It meant that I wasn't alone. It meant that nothing was

---

*It turns out that while neo-pronouns can be exhausting, they can also be illuminating.

wrong with me. I had this same feeling—revelation—when I learned about bisexuality's validity. And I had the same sense of relief when I learned that other folks shared in some of my more aggressive kinks.

But it wasn't just feeling "normal" that alleviated my concerns. I could finally take action. Instead of looking for the unknown cause of my (lack of) sexual desires with my romantic partners, I could focus on having a fulfilling sex life with a bunch of different folks. It meant that I could have a romantic partner whom I don't have sex with often—and that it wasn't an indicator something was "wrong" with our relationship, but simply reflective of my personal relationship with sex.

I've realized that sex has always been about the novelty for me. It's never been an extension of my love for my partners or how I bond with them. I'd much rather cuddle and watch a movie with my partner than have sex with them. Having deep heart-to-hearts is how I connect with partners. It's why my love for Evan, my straight best friend, is stronger than that for many of my romantic and sexual partners. We get tipsy and have long heart-to-hearts until the sunrise.

I still talk to Cooper, not infrequently. He sends me memes almost daily, but we don't talk about anything too deep. Although, when I visit my brother in San Francisco I always see Cooper. We usually stay up until seven in the morning talking about our lives. Last time, even though I slept over, I was afraid to cuddle him. As if cuddling him would lead to sex, and I would be "triggered." I'm embarrassed to admit that I was stiff as a board when we fell asleep beside each other.

But we love each other. We always will. And he'll always have a special place in my heart as my first boyfriend, the first person to introduce me to polyamory, and the first partner with whom I could be brutally honest.

X X X

Whenever it comes up that I'm polyamorous, many are quick to say they could never be. I was them once, before Cooper. Until I was ethically non-monogamous (ENM), I never realized how much of an awkward and egocentric response that is. You're answering a question that was never asked. It's like, I'm glad you know that about yourself, but what do you want me to say? Well, now I respond, "I don't think I could ever go back to being monogamous."

I don't think ENM is superior or more "natural" than monogamy, or vice versa. Neither do I think one is "easier" than the other. Both come with an array of unique challenges. Some people are simply better suited to the problems that come with one over the other.

Generally, I think people attracted to multiple or all genders are better suited for ENM, and that's why they identify as poly significantly more than straight folks. A 2019 study published in the *Journal of Sex Research* compared the demographic backgrounds of 2,428 polyamorous individuals and 539 monogamous ones by asking participants to take an online survey. The big takeaways from the research were that polyamorous people tend to identify more as bisexual/pansexual, are more likely to report being divorced, and make less money yearly than monogamous couples.*

I think some bi people, not all, miss being with other genders when monogamous—but there's more to it. Polyamory is very affirming to bi folks' identity. As I've discussed, when monogamous, you can't be in a "bi" relationship; you're a man dating a man or a man dating a woman (or any number of other combinations that, to the rest of the world, simply *look* gay or straight, with very little obvious nuance). When you're poly, you can simultaneously have a

---

*Participants in poly relationships were significantly more likely to make less than $20,000 a year, and those in monogamous relationships were more likely to make $100,000 per year, opposing the idea that all polyamorous folks are bored, rich suburbanites.

boyfriend, girlfriend, and theyfriend to boot, and that's *really* fucking bisexual. You are perceived and believed to be bisexual because you have partners of different genders. Again, very affirming. It's also affirming to not feel like you're picking a team. You can go to the Eagle with your boyfriend and a Dodgers game with your wife (or whatever straight people like to do—I don't know, maybe some of your wives like going to the Eagle).

I've spoken to many experts about the "trade-off" when choosing poly or mono. Many say ENM allows for more freedom, independence, exploration, and novelty, whereas monogamy provides more stability and security.

Maybe this is (often) true—but I'm not sure those benefits are inherent. In other words, I believe you *can* have a very secure polyamorous relationship as you date and love multiple people. You can have independence and novelty within a monogamous relationship, too. There are plenty of people who feel insecure in monogamous relationships—think of everyone who's afraid of their partner cheating or leaving them. Then there are folks who feel trapped in polyamory. This often occurs when a primary partner attempts to control their behavior (e.g., whom they can date and fuck).

Psychotherapist Jessica Fern sums this up nicely in her book, *Polysecure*, which I highly recommend. She notes that people tend to rely "too much on the structure of the relationship to ensure and safe-guard secure attachment instead of the quality of relating between partners to forge secure attachment."

She continues, "When we rely on the structure of our relationship, whether that is through being monogamous with someone or practicing hierarchical forms of CNM, we run the risk of forgetting that secure attachment is an embodied expression built upon how we consistently respond and attune to each other, not something that gets created through structure and hierarchy."

Countless marriages end in divorce. Monogamous people cheat all the goddamn time. Evidently, the secure safeguards of monogamy don't help all that much. You *can* cheat while in an ethically non-monogamous relationship—breaking the rules of your open agreement or lying about having sex with someone—but poly people are significantly less likely to cheat. The whole point is that you don't have to cheat.

Alas, human beings *love* to project. Monogamous people assume since they couldn't ever be poly, that means polyamory doesn't work. This is disheartening but expected. Alternative lifestyles are demonized because they threaten the status quo. Ironically, alt people take so much pride in being alternative that the last thing on their minds is conversion. They like being different from the status quo.

While I find it discouraging when (certain) mono people disparage poly people, I become enraged when poly people attack monogamous folks. For example, there's a select group of polyamorous men who insist on reminding you that only a handful of animals mate for life; therefore, monogamy is "unnatural." Okay, but what about the 5 percent of animals that do remain sexually and romantically monogamous—how do you explain them? And while humans may be animals, we're a *bit* more complex than that. Frankly, I don't care about the relationship structure of hippopotami. Unless a hippo also has to respond to a hundred emails a day and is worried about how it's going to pay rent, I'm not modeling my relationship after a goddamn hippo.

Then there are the folks who say monogamy, or more specifically marriage, is a patriarchal and sexist institution. To that I say you're right, but, *meh*. While undeniably *rooted* in a patriarchal system, that doesn't mean marriage *has* to be now. If you and your spouse are egalitarian and treat each other with respect, then marriage and monogamy can be modern, even radical.

I think the only somewhat valid critique of monogamy is that it affords a pleasant lack of self-awareness and introspection that anyone, but monogamists the most, take for granted. Monogamous people live in a sort of fantasyland where they don't have to be introspective. They don't have to interrogate their struggles with jealousy, abandonment, or control. They can very easily say, "Eh, not a good fit," and move along. Per Fern's comments, they rely on the relationship structure to keep their relationship secure, and doing so inhibits personal growth. That's why some poly people pity monogamous folks. They feel bad because they know that many monogamous folks' glass houses would shatter if, say, their boyfriend got drunk and made the small and innocuous mistake of making out with someone else.

Still, I don't think this gives poly people the right to condescend. And of course, #notallmonogamists. There are plenty of fulfilled monogamous couples where both people are introspective and aren't relying on the structure of the relationship. I fully support these folks. You all are killing it!

At the end of the day, I just want you to have the relationship structure you'd like without any pressure from your friends, family, partner(s), or society at large. I want that for me, too. Don't be monogamous just because your mom thinks polyamory is invalid, and don't open up your relationship because your boyfriend said, "It's 2023. Every gay couple is open now."

You can and should find a partner who desires and thrives in the same relationship structure as you, no matter how "unique" your desires are. Take me. I'm a bisexual, polyamorous kinkster with an insatiable sexual appetite, but because I'm on the fraysexual spectrum, I have little desire to have sex with my romantic partners. It may seem like I'd never be able to have a serious boyfriend, girlfriend, or they-friend because of the complexities of my identity and desires, but I do. I have my boyfriend Jordan (if he hasn't broken up with me yet). Our relationship works because he is a porn star, so he literally has sex with men far hotter than me all day, every day. By the time he sees me, he's typically not in the mood to fuck. He just got railed by a ten-incher on set for the past six hours and came three times.

I'm not the only one who gets something out of our relationship. He loves and appreciates that I'm supportive of him and his work. Most people refuse to date a porn star, or they try to but quickly become threatened by all the dick their partner takes. They then proceed to act out and drama ensues. Not me. I don't get jealous or worried. I love the fact he gets to fuck hot dudes daily because it takes pressure off me to fuck him. Everyone wins here!*

Find what works for you. Figure out a relationship structure with your partner(s) that gives you security and novelty. There's no rule-book for how your relationship needs to function. The only rule is to be honest with yourself and your partners about your needs and desires, and to be receptive to theirs. You probably won't end up with a hot porn star boyfriend, but at the very least you'll end up in relationship(s) where you thrive.

---

*And I *really* win when he invites me to shoot for his OnlyFans, and we tag-team a porn star I've had a crush on for years.

CHAPTER 15

BISLUT

I n 2016, right after becoming official boyfriends, Cooper and I attended a bisexual meetup for men. While we were enmeshed in our queer, poly community, our lives still suffered from a dearth of other bi men. There were fluid and heteroflexible guys—guys who felt comfortable making out with other dudes and getting the off blow job, as long as his peen was also getting sucked by a chick—but we knew few other openly bi men who actually wanted to go to a gay bar with us to watch *Drag Race* (and fuck some dudes after).

So Cooper and I decided to head to this bi men's meetup in Boston. We were excited to meet new guys like us and to bring some bi men into our polycule. But our excitement plummeted the moment we stepped through the doors and into a classroom that gave off dreary AA vibes. Tables were pushed to the sides of the room, and there were about ten seats arranged in a circle. Three seats were taken. Two by very unassuming men who did not appear visibly queer. They looked like they worked in construction with their baggy jeans, flannel shirts, and long neckbeards. The third seat was taken by a young man, in his late twenties, who I learned was the discussion leader—though the discussion didn't need much leading.

The two fortysomethings were newly out as bisexual, or rather, they had admitted to themselves that they were bi, but hardly anyone in their lives knew. They had no idea what it "meant" to be bi and how they could meet other gay/bi men. I don't think these guys even knew what Grindr was, and it didn't seem like they'd heard of the concept of a gay bar, let alone were planning to join us for *Drag Race*.

They were lonely. They needed friends—a community—or else they'd likely spend the rest of their lives partially closeted, never feeling like they belonged. Selfishly, I was heartbroken, or perhaps, more accurately, discouraged. *These guys were the only two attendees who showed up to the meetup? Was this all there was for bi men? Was there absolutely zero community for us?* Cooper and I hustled out of the room the moment the meeting ended and vowed to never return.

X X X

Even though I don't try to, I often think about that day. I think about it when I'm in a gay bar and don't feel comfortable kissing my girlfriend. I think about it when questioning why there are hardly any bisexual-specific spaces. I think about it when I feel split between the "straight" and "gay" worlds.

For years I wished there was a space for me, and with the increased amount of bi visibility, I figured something would eventually emerge. But by 2022, there still wasn't much for bi men, even at sex parties, where sex-positivity ran rampant. Every "queer" sex party I had ever attended had women who hooked up with other women and men who hooked up with women. Never guy-on-guy action. Never MMM, MMF, or my personal favorite, MFFMMFMMFFFM. Yet the party promoters had the gall to call these parties queer—fake news!

Now the lack of man-on-man action wasn't due to these men being straight. Many bi men attend queer sex parties, but few bi guys feel comfortable hooking up with men in front of women. I understand why. Many of us have been rejected by (cis) women when we share that we're bi, for any number of reasons. This repeated rejection stays with us. We begin to think we're undesirable in the eyes of women. I couldn't tell you the number of times things had been going well with a woman only for them to ghost after learning I was bi.

For all these reasons and more, I decided to create a sex party focused on bi men and their admirers.

I wanted a space where a bi guy wearing seven-inch Pleasers, Fenty lip gloss, a Marek+Richard's crop, and an Andrew Christian thong could get spit-roasted by his girlfriend's strap-on and some stranger's dick. I wanted a space where a gold-star gay could tell a woman, "You know, I've never had sex with a woman before, but would like to try with you," and she'd respond, "This is my dream come true." I wanted a space where bi trans men felt openly desired by cis guys. Do you know who doesn't give a fuck about your genitals? Bi people. We love it all!

I was being the change I wanted to see in the world. (Am I a bisexual Gandhi? Yes, yes, I am.) I knew that I wasn't special; if I desperately needed a bi man–centric space, then other bi men did, too.

In April 2022, it happened. I created, produced, threw, hosted, and performed at my party, aptly named Bislut. Bislut was the sex party I had always wanted to throw. Unlike other parties I'd produced, it wasn't exclusively for those who identified as men. Bislut specifically catered to those seeking sexual encounters with men, women, and nonbinary folks in a single space.

By the time April rolled around, I had done everything in my power to make sure the event was welcoming, safe, inclusive, and raunchy as all hell. I wrote a consent speech for the angel working the door to read to each attendee. I informed the consent guardians (i.e., those who monitor the play space and the rest of the party to make sure no one was being a creep) of exactly what I needed them to do and how to respond to hypothetical scenarios. The projector was on with trippy visuals. The DJ had sets for upstairs (dance music) and downstairs (sex music). The bar was stocked, the food was beautifully displayed, the coat checker knew when to give out the branded merch goodie bags, and the performance space was cleared, so I, along with my close friend Torro Royale, could perform our numbers.

I micromanaged everything until two minutes before guests arrived. Then I took a deep breath and mentally prepared to transition into host mode. There were more than 150 people slated to attend—all of them would know who I was.

People arrived right on time, and by eleven, more than a hundred people were already there. For a party that would go until five in the morning, I was shocked by how many people arrived right as the doors opened—but hey, bi people are horny.

I casually mingled for the first hour and a half. A man wearing a harness over his shirt came up to me while holding a woman's hand. He introduced himself nervously and said, "You have no idea how monumental your work has been to my life. I was able to come out to my wife," he said, smiling at the person whose hand he was holding. "And our relationship has never been stronger."

I started tearing up as I thanked him profusely for sharing. I had two other similar encounters that night. Each time, I cried with joy.

By the time we closed the doors at midnight, everyone was in attendance. Standing on the mini-stage, I thanked everyone for coming. "For a long time, I've wanted a space that isn't just inclusive of bi men but also celebrates us. I wanted a place where we felt empowered and encouraged to be our most unabashed sexual selves with our partners of all genders. So thank you, I could not have done this without you here."

I then introduced Goddess Torro Royale, who performed a burlesque routine where she seductively tantalized the audience. She slowly stripped down each layer until she ended her performance by riding her boyfriend's face. Absolutely everyone wanted to fuck her by the time she finished her number.

Afterward, I strutted to the stage wearing an elaborate leather harness-garter that wrapped around my every curve, and a one-of-a-kind yellow "caution" jockstrap, revealing my furry booty. My first performance was to Kim Petras' song "Slut Pop"—only I had a friend edit the audio, so every time she sang "Slut Pop," we instead heard "Bislut."*

This is Bislut, whip your dick out
Turn your bitch out, out, out, out-out-out-out

I half lip-synced, half sung. I spread my cheeks and sat on the staircase banister. I rode it like a cowboy and the crowd went wild, but not nearly as wild as when I performed my second number, "Throat Goat," another song on Petras' newest album. I sang the first verse:

I can take it all, love it big or small
Make it hit the wall, I'm the throat goat

That's when two men and a woman joined the stage. The men wore nothing but sexy undies, and the woman wore a strap-on. I removed the men's briefs and started to deepthroat their dicks along with the strap-on. For two minutes straight, I gagged on that shit like the champion I was. When the song was over, I wiped the saliva off my beard and said, "All right, I think it's time to start fucking!"

The horny Bisluts did not hesitate. Within minutes, the three bedrooms on the first floor were packed with people rubbing up against each other. The downstairs basement, which consisted of ten queen beds, was full. There were nude bodies as far as the eye could see. Dicks, tits, pussies, asses, and strap-ons out with every configuration of bisexual sex you could possibly imagine. Men were not shying away from being sexual with other guys, and women were pouncing at the opportunity to share a dick with a bi boy.

---

*For legal reasons, we can't publish more than two lines from the song, but if you are unfamiliar, *please* Google "Slut Pop Kim Petras lyrics."

I stood in the center of all the action and slowly turned to take in each scene. My hands covered my mouth in joyous disbelief. I had never been a part of anything like this before on such a large scale. The space I wanted, I needed, for as long as I could remember, finally existed. If I had died at that moment—which was a possibility because I was so aroused—I would have died happy.

X X X

It's easy to reduce the Bislut party, or even this book, to solely sex. But that would miss the point. Parties, books, and all types of queer media and representation are not just about sex but about what sex influences—which is everything.

How much of our lives are dedicated to our sexual relationships? How often do people break up for sex-related issues: wanting too much sex, too little sex, not being able to orgasm, not getting hard, having painful sex, not having satisfying sex, being sexually incompatible, yearning for wild kinks, and not being able to embrace same-sex sex? How much time have we spent on the apps? How many times have we cheated or been cheated on? How often have we felt used for sex or used others for sex? How often do normal, healthy sexual desires make us feel shame? How often does this shame lead to anxiety, depression, drug abuse, and alcoholism? How often does our shame cause us to angrily project our insecurities onto others? How often do we get our feelings hurt because someone we like doesn't want to have sex with us? How much time and money have we spent in therapy discussing our love and sex lives?

The way society has conceptualized and taught sex has made *all* of our lives worse, regardless of gender and sexual orientation. The heteronormative hunter/hunted dynamic helps no one; it's only made masculinity more toxic and exacerbated male privilege, enabling men to keep treating women horribly. And the notion that a woman's value goes down because she's had a lot of sex whereas a man's goes up? Ridiculous. Our value shouldn't be correlated to sex.

Then there's the fact that our language around sex and sexual dynamics is often exclusionary of nonbinary people, and that's by design. Nonbinary people transcend gender stereotypes, so there's no place for them in conversations among those who perpetuate the idea that "men are from Mars" and "women are from Venus."

Don't think you're off society's hook if you're a man who only dates and fucks other men. All too often, you'll see jokes about "top" privilege on social media. Yes, it's a funny bit, but it is rooted in common and unsettling relationship dynamics among queer men. The top, which in this case is synonymous with being the more "masculine" partner, can treat the bottom, the more submissive partner, like an object (not in the hot "I'm just a hole" kinda way) because of what? Goddamn male privilege. In this sense, men who sleep with men are also conditioned by these same heteronormative sexual dynamics that plague everyone's romantic lives. We all know that one guy who exclusively tops and expects "his" bottom to be constantly at the ready. He's emotionally stunted and avoids commitment like the plague; in this way, he shares even more with straight men than with other gay men.*

If you don't have sex, or are asexual, sex still influences your life. When you're asexual, you have to claim an identity that proclaims your lack of desire for sex. That's how monumental sex is. That's because sex bleeds out into platonic relationships with our parents, siblings, bosses, teachers, and non-sex friends. Everything is connected, so we can't compartmentalize our sexual relationships, even if we try. The shame we feel in the bedroom seeps into our everyday lives. We lash

---

*If you're this type of top, only use bottoms who WANT to be used. There are plenty of them. But also work on your top privilege, too.

out at the people we love. We withdraw. We hide crucial elements of who we are. We lose the ability to trust and build connections.

This is why I'm so brazen when I talk about sex. We *need* to be able to talk about it openly. Recently I've seen a de-emphasis on sex when discussing sexuality, especially bisexuality. I think we hope that this neutered form of visibility makes us more palatable to a sex-negative, mainstream audience. But that doesn't benefit anyone. Not talking about something that we all do isn't going to solve anything. We've attempted to sweep sex under the rug for centuries, and look where that's gotten us.

Sex isn't going away anytime soon. In fact, it's one of the few things that have remained constant since the dawn of humankind. Our existence depends on it. Yet, we are still terrible at talking about it. Weirdly, we're worse at talking about sex than actually having it.

So however you like to have sex, own it. If you're a Boyslut who takes anonymous loads at the sauna every day of the week that ends in "day," live your truth. If you only sleep with a select few once you have a romantic connection, do that. If you only want to have non-penetrative sex, then remind yourself (and your partners) that non-penetrative sex "counts." Don't feel pressured to stick your dick into anything or to fill up all your holes.

When you own your sexual desires and have a satisfying sex life—however that looks to you—your life can feel more balanced, and your community can feel richer. The only thing better than being a sex-positive Boyslut is surrounding yourself with other sex-positive Boysluts who make you feel appreciated, loved, and embraced.

It's hard opening up about yourself when you know you'll be judged. It's hard to embrace who you are when you fear rejection. It's hard to grow as a person when you're simply trying to survive. That's why it's necessary to have a community—and when I say community, this can mean a close-knit friend group—where you're encouraged to be authentically you. The Bislut party created a sex-positive, bisexual, non-monogamous community that hadn't existed. It didn't exist when my psychiatrist told me that men cannot be bisexual. It didn't exist when I first Googled "bisexual man," and it didn't exist when I attended the bi men's meetup in Boston that made me want to jump back into the closet. But it exists now.

For the first time in centuries, I think the world is ready for the communicative, openly sexual, nontoxic Boyslut. Even if the world isn't ready, it doesn't matter. We'll be so loud talking about sex that everyone will have to listen.

BIBLIOGRAPHY

GLOSSARY

Engle, Gigi. "If a Couple Wants to 'Soft Swap' with You, Here's What It Means." *Men's Health*, October 15, 2021. https://www.menshealth.com/sex-women/a37973022/soft-swap-vs-full-swap/.

"FDA Approves First Injectable Treatment for HIV Pre-Exposure Prevention." FDA, 2021. http://www.fda.gov/news-events/press-announcements/fda-approves-first-injectable-treatment-hiv-pre-exposure-prevention.

Ochs, Robyn. "Bisexual." 2014. https://robynochs.com/bisexual/.

"PrEP." Centers for Disease Control and Prevention. 2019. http://cdc.gov/hiv/basics/prep.html.

Zane, Zachary. "Here's How to Tell If You're Fraysexual." *Men's Health*, February 14, 2022. https://www.menshealth.com/sex-women/a39051414/fraysexual-meaning/.

Zane, Zachary. "What's the Real Difference between Bi- and Pansexual?" *Rolling Stone*, June 29, 2018. https://www.rollingstone.com/culture/culture-features/whats-the-real-difference-between-bi-and-pansexual-667087/.

CHAPTER 1

Allen, Samantha. "Why Amber Rose Won't Date Bisexual Men—and Why She's Wrong." The Daily Beast, April 11, 2017. https://www.thedailybeast.com/why-amber-rose-wont-date-bisexual-menand-why-shes-wrong.

"I Keep Having Intrusive Thoughts about Murdering and Torturing My Daughter and It's Ruining My Life." Reddit, 2014. https://www.reddit.com/r/TwoXChromosomes/comments/3cn1a4/i_keep_having_intrusive_thoughts_about_murdering/.

CHAPTER 2

Van Boom, Daniel. "Porn Addiction Is Ruining Lives, but Scientists Aren't Convinced It's Real." CNET, December 1, 2020. https://www.cnet.com/culture/features/porn-addiction-is-ruining-lives-but-scientists-arent-convinced-its-real/.

CHAPTER 3

"A Closer Look: Bisexual Transgender People." Movement Advancement Project. https://www.lgbtmap.org/bisexual-transgender.

Frieden, Thomas R., Linda C. Degutis, Howard R. Spivak, Mikel L. Walters, Jieru Chen, and Jackhew J. Breiding. "The National Intimate Partner and Sexual Violence Survey: 2010 Findings on Victimization by Sexual Orientation." National Center for Injury Prevention and Control, Division of Violence Prevention, 2012. https://www.cdc.gov/violenceprevention/pdf/nisvs_sofindings.pdf.

Hottes, Travis Salway, Laura Bogaert, Anne E. Rhodes, David J. Brennan, and Dionne Gesink. "Lifetime Prevalence of Suicide Attempts among Sexual Minority Adults by Study Sampling Strategies: A Systematic Review and Meta-Analysis." *American Journal of Public Health* 106, no. 5 (2016): e1–12. https://doi .org/10.2105/ajph.2016.303088.

Hottes, Travis Salway, Olivier Ferlatte, and Dionne Gesink. "Suicide and HIV as Leading Causes of Death among Gay and Bisexual Men: A Comparison of Estimated Mortality and Published Research." *Critical Public Health* 25, no. 5 (2014): 513–26. https://doi.org /10.1080/09581596.2014.946887.

"LGBTQ Youth and Suicide." NYC Department of Health. https://www1.nyc.gov /site/doh/health/health-topics/lgbtq-youth -suicide.page.

Schuler, Megan S., and Rebecca L. Collins. "Sexual Minority Substance Use Disparities: Bisexual Women at Elevated Risk Relative to Other Sexual Minority Groups." *Drug and Alcohol Dependence* 206 (January 2020): 107755. https://doi .org/10.1016/j.drugalcdep .2019.107755.

CHAPTER 4

"Substance Use among Gay and Bisexual Men." CDC, 2020. https://www.cdc.gov /msmhealth/substance-abuse.htm.

CHAPTER 5

Eisenberger, Naomi. "Why Rejection Hurts: What Social Neuroscience Has Revealed about the Brain's Response to Social Rejection." 2016. https://sanlab.psych.ucla .edu/wp-content/uploads/sites/31/2015/05/39 -Decety-39.pdf.

Eisenberger, Naomi I., Johanna M. Jarcho, Jackhew D. Lieberman, and Bruce D. Naliboff. "An Experimental Study of Shared Sensitivity to Physical Pain and Social Rejection." *Pain* 126, no. 1 (2006): 132–38. https://doi .org/10.1016/j.pain.2006.06.024.

CHAPTER 6

Carey, Benedict. "Straight, Gay or Lying? Bisexuality Revisited." *New York Times*, July 5, 2005. https://www.nytimes.com/2005/07/05 /health/straight-gay-or-lying -bisexuality -revisited.html.

"Normative Male Alexithymia." American Psychological Association. https://dictionary .apa.org/normative-male-alexithymia.

Rieger, G., M. L. Chivers, and J. M. Bailey. "Sexual Arousal Patterns of Bisexual Men." *Psychological Science* 16, no. 8 (2005): 579–84. https://doi.org/10.1111/j.1467 –9280.2005.01578.x.

Rosenthal, A. M., D. Sylva, A. Safron, and J. M. Bailey. "Sexual Arousal Patterns of Bisexual Men Revisited." *Biological Psychology* 88, no. 1 (2011): 112–15. https://doi.org/10.1016/j .biopsycho.2011.06.015.

Tuller, David. "No Surprise for Bisexual Men: Report Indicates They Exist." *New York Times*, August 22, 2011. https:// www.nytimes.com/2011/08/23 /health/23bisexual.html.

CHAPTER 8

Assuncao, Muri. "Freelancers Claim They Haven't Been Paid for Contributions to Out Magazine." *Daily News* (New York), February 27, 2019. https://www.nydailynews .com/news/national/ny-news-out-magazine -nwu-20190226-story.html.

Avery, Dan. "Bisexual Men More Prone to Eating Disorders than Gay or Straight Men, Study Finds." NBC News, December 18, 2020. https://www.nbcnews.com/feature /nbc-out/bisexual-men-more-prone -eating-disorders-gay-or-straight-men -n1251626.

Ballard, Jamie. "More Young Americans Now Identify as Bisexual." YouGov, June 18, 2018. https://today.yougov.com/topics/lifestyle /articles-reports/2018/06/18/more-young -americans-now-identify-bisexual.

Dahlgreen, Will, and Anna-Elizabeth Shakespeare. "1 in 2 Young People Say They Are Not 100% Heterosexual." YouGov, August 16, 2015. https://yougov.co.uk/topics /lifestyle/articles-reports/2015/08/16/half -young-not-heterosexual.

Katz-Wise, Sabra L., Ethan H. Mereish, and Julie Woulfe. "Associations of Bisexual-Specific Minority Stress and Health among Cisgender and Transgender Adults with Bisexual Orientation." *Journal of Sex Research* 54, no. 7 (2016): 899–910. https://doi.org /10.1080/00224499.2016.1236181.

Moore, Peter. "A Third of Young Americans Say They Aren't 100% Heterosexual." YouGov, August 20, 2015. https://today .yougov.com/topics/lifestyle/articles -reports/2015/08/20/third-young-americans -exclusively-heterosexual.

Ochs, Robyn. "Bisexuality Has Always Challenged Norms—Even in the Queer World." *Nation,* June 29, 2019. https://www .thenation.com/article/archive/stonewall -bisexuality-lgbtq-exclusion/.

Pompili, Maurizio, David Lester, Alberto Forte, Maria Elena Seretti, Denise Erbuto, Dorian A. Lamis, Mario Amore, and

Paolo Girardi. "Bisexuality and Suicide: A Systematic Review of the Current Literature." *Journal of Sexual Medicine* 11, no. 8 (2014): 1903–13. https://doi.org/10.1111 /jsm.12581.

Rhodes, Martha. "A Short History of the Word 'Bisexuality.'" Stonewall, January 31, 2022. https://www.stonewall.org.uk/about-u /news/short-history-word-bisexuality.

Ross, Lori E., Travis Salway, Lesley A. Tarasoff, Jenna M. MacKay, Blake W. Hawkins, and Charles P. Fehr. "Prevalence of Depression and Anxiety among Bisexual People Compared to Gay, Lesbian, and Heterosexual Individuals: A Systematic Review and Meta-Analysis." *Journal of Sex Research* 55, nos. 4–5 (2017): 435–56. https:// doi.org/10.1080/00224499.2017.1387755.

Zane, Zachary. "I Don't Know Who Needs to Hear This, but You Are Bi Enough." *New York Times,* June 17, 2021. http://www.nytimes .com/2021/06/17/opinion/bisexuals -coming-out-anna-paquin.html.

Zane, Zachary. "In the LGBT Community, Bisexual People Have More Health Risks. Here's What Could Help." *Washington Post*, September 25, 2017. https://www .washingtonpost.com/news/soloish /wp/2017/09/25/in-the-lgbt-community -bisexual-people-have-more-health-risks -heres-what-could-help/.

CHAPTER 9

de Klerk, Amy. "These Are the Apps That Are Making You Unhappy." *Harper's Bazaar*, September 4, 2017. https://www .harpersbazaar.com/uk/culture/culture -news/a43619/apps-bad-for-mood/.

Jones, Jeffrey. "LGBT Americans Married to Same-Sex Spouse Steady at 10%." Gallup, 2022. https://news.gallup.com/poll/389555 /lgbt-americans-married-same-sex-spouse -steady.aspx.

Morgan, Jacob. "The Top 10 Factors for On-the-Job Employee Happiness." *Forbes*, December 15, 2014. https://www.forbes.com /sites/jacobmorgan/2014/12/15/the-top-10 -factors-for-on-the-job-employee -happiness/?sh=7353cd595afa.

Wakefield, Lily. "Grindr Killer Stephen Port and the Horrific Murder Spree That Devastated a Nation." PinkNews, January 3, 2022. https://www.pinknews.co.uk/2022 /01/03/stephen-port-grindr-killer-murder -four-lives/.

CHAPTER 11

Cascalheira, Cory J., Ellen E. Ijebor, Yelena Salkowitz, Tracie L. Hitter, and Allison Boyce. "Curative Kink: Survivors of Early Abuse Transform Trauma through BDSM." *Sexual and Relationship Therapy*, June 2021: 1–31. https://doi.org/10.1080/14681994.2021 .1937599.

Lehmiller, Justin J. *Tell Me What You Want: The Science of Sexual Desire and How It Can Help You Improve Your Sex Life.* New York: Da Capo Lifelong Books, 2018.

Taylor, Jordyn, and Zachary Zane. *Men's Health Best. Sex. Ever.: 200 Frank, Funny & Friendly Answers about Getting It On.* New York: Hearst Home Books, 2022.

CHAPTER 12

"FDA Approves First Drug for Reducing the Risk of Sexually Acquired HIV Infection."

HIV.gov, July 16, 2012. https://www.hiv.gov /blog/fda-approves-first-drug-for-reducing -the-risk-of-sexually-acquired-hiv-infection.

Frith, John. "Syphilis—Its Early History and Treatment until Penicillin and the Debate on Its Origins." *Journal of Military and Veterans Health* 20, no. 4 (2011). https://jmvh .org/article/syphilis-its-early-history-and -treatment-until-penicillin-and-the-debate -on-its-origins/.

"Genital Herpes Screening." CDC, 2019. https:// www.cdc.gov/std/herpes/screening.htm.

Hartley, Charlotte. "Medieval DNA Suggests Columbus Didn't Trigger Syphilis Epidemic in Europe." *Science*, August 13, 2020. https:// www.science.org/content/article/medieval -dna-suggests-columbus-didn-t-trigger -syphilis-epidemic-europe.

"HIV/AIDS." World Health Organization, 2021. https://www.who.int/data/gho/data /themes/hiv-aids.

"New Data Suggest STDs Continued to Increase During First Year of the COVID-19 Pandemic." CDC, 2022. https://www.cdc.gov /media/releases/2022/p0412-STD-Increase .html.

"PrEP Effectiveness." CDC, 2022. https:// www.cdc.gov/hiv/basics/prep/prep -effectiveness.html.

Rosenfeld, Dana. "The AIDS Epidemic's Lasting Impact on Gay Men." British Academy, February 19, 2018. https://www .thebritishacademy.ac.uk/blog/aids -epidemic-lasting-impact-gay-men/.

"Sexually Transmitted Disease Surveillance." CDC, 2015. https://www.cdc.gov/std /stats/archive/STD-Surveillance-2015-print.pdf.

Tampa, M., I. Sarbu, C. Matei, V. Benea, and S. R. Georgescu. "Brief History of Syphilis." *Journal of Medicine and Life* 7, no. 1 (2014): 4–10. https://www.ncbi.nlm.nih.gov/pmc /articles/PMC3956094/.

"The HIV/AIDS Epidemic in the United States: The Basics." Kaiser Family Foundation, 2021. https://www.kff.org /hivaids/fact-sheet/the-hivaids-epidemic -in-the-united-states-the-basics/.

CHAPTER 14

Balzarini, Rhonda N., Christoffer Dharma, Taylor Kohut, Bjarne M. Holmes, Lorne Campbell, Justin J. Lehmiller, and Jennifer J. Harman. "Demographic Comparison of American Individuals in Polyamorous and Monogamous Relationships." *Journal of Sex Research* 56, no. 6 (2018): 681–94. https://do.org/10.1080/00224499.2018 .1474333.

Fern, Jessica. *Polysecure: Attachment, Trauma and Consensual Nonmonogamy.* Portland, OR: Thorntree Press, 2020.

Harmon, Katherine. "Love for Life? 12 Animals That Are (Mostly) Monogamous." *Scientific American*, February 14, 2012. http:// scientificamerican.com/article/love-for-life -animals-mostly-monogamous/.

ACKNOWLEDGMENTS

Imagine if I said, "There is no one I would like to acknowledge. This was all me, baby!" Well, that would be a big, fat lie because *Boyslut* would not exist without the support and encouragement of so many incredible people.

First off, I have to thank my uncle Ken, who probably looked at ten iterations of the proposal, each time pushing me to dig deeper. You also came up *with* Boyslut—the word, the title, my goddamn identity! I bet you didn't think it would lead to this!

I'd also like to thank my sister-in-law, Taylor. You read my first novel when I was twenty-three. It was *garbage*. I had six pages describing the protagonist picking his nose. Still, you sat down with me and went page-by-page, giving me not just edits but hope that I could one day become a published author.

To Jordyn Taylor, my editor at *Men's Health*, you've taught me how to hone my writing over the years and took a chance by giving me, a flaming bisexual man, a sex advice column at *Men's*—freaking—*Health*!

Of course, I want to thank my family: my brothers Alex and Niko, my sisters-in-law Sonia and Taylor (again), my grandma Sally, Mom, and Dad. You've heard me talk about this book incessantly and have had to listen to me question whether I should put all this private information about myself into the world. (Welp, it's out there. Sorry, Rose!) Then, after all our talks, I forbade you from reading the book. (I'm serious. Do not read it!)

To my editor Zack Knoll, you knew *exactly* which questions to ask to bring out the best of me and my writing. I looked at the first draft I submitted and compared it to where we are now, and it's a world of difference. Katherine Latshaw, my ball-busting agent, you believed in this project from day one. Many of the other agents I submitted to were *confused . . . offended . . . bewildered?* Not you!

To my poly group, HOME, I love you guys. You're my chosen family, and you have supported the *shit* out of me, giving me delusional confidence. To Melissa and Sophie, where would I be without our group chat and your unconditional support?

And I want to thank every single one of you who has read my work for years and kept pushing me to keep writing, even—especially—when I was getting death threats. (The internet is a wonderful place!) Your support and encouragement were how I pushed through. I mean that.

Last but not least, I want to thank you, the reader, who bought this book. (Please tell me you bought it and didn't borrow it from a friend.) I really hope *Boyslut* positively impacts your life, and you can move through this crazy world with a little less sexual shame than you did before. And please, for the love of God, send nudes.

Xoxo,
The Boyslut

ABOUT THE AUTHOR

ZACHARY ZANE is a Brooklyn-based columnist, sex expert, and activist whose work focuses on sexuality, lifestyle, culture, and the LGBTQ community. He currently has a sex advice column at *Men's Health* titled Sexplain It.

His work has been published in the *New York Times, Rolling Stone*, the *Washington Post, GQ, Playboy*, Slate, *Cosmo*, Bustle, Vice, NBC News, *Dazed*, the Daily Beast, and many others. He is the founder and editor-in-chief of *BOYSLUT* zine, which publishes nonfiction sex stories from kinksters across the globe, and is also the co-author of the sex advice book *Men's Health: Best. Sex. Ever.*

He was formerly a digital associate editor at *OUT* magazine and a contributing editor at Pride.com, *Plus* magazine, and *The Advocate* magazine. As a leading bisexual activist, Zane has spoken across the country at universities and panels alike, discussing issues pertaining to the bisexual community, sex-positivity, and ethical non-monogamy. He attended the Bisexual White House Briefing at the White House (under Obama) and has been featured as an expert on a number of podcasts, including Dan Savage's *Savage Lovecast*.